IN EDINBURGH—NOW!

IN EDINBURGH—NOW!

PAGES FROM A SUBURBAN NOTE-BOOK

By

JEAN M. SPEEDY

THE QUOTA PRESS

BELFAST

1930

First Published   -   -   -   *November* 1930
Second Impression -   -   -   *December* 1930

PRINTED IN GUERNSEY, C.I., BRITISH ISLES,
BY THE STAR AND GAZETTE COMPANY LTD.

To Mother

The majority of these articles have appeared in the *Weekly Scotsman*, two of them in *The Scotsman*, and one in the *Edinburgh Evening Dispatch* : to the proprietors and the respective editors I am indebted for permission to reprint them. Three of them have not previously been published.

CONTENTS

I

"MINE OWN ROMANTIC TOWN!"

II

THE ROUND OF THE YEAR

CONTENTS *(Continued)*

III

IN PENSIVE VEIN

INTRODUCTION

OUR road near the Braid Hills rises steeply from the tram-line, securing for us a lofty vantage point from which to view our beloved city and her surrounding hills.

From our front windows we look, over the roofs of the newly-fledged bungalows, to the long undulating line of the Pentlands, their grassy smoothness broken only by that rough scaur above Swanston. Nearly always are these " Hills of Home " willing to refresh our eyes, varying their colours from the grey of morning to the green, blue-misted, of summer afternoons; from autumn's brown, warm and intimate, to winter's white, when the T plantation stands out more darkly impressed on its snowy background. When the mists blot out the hills we feel as though a friend has withdrawn from us.

Our back windows peer across the breadth of the city to a blue streak of the Firth of Forth and to the hills of Fife beyond. Craiglockhart Hills, on the one side, the Braids on the other, take a peep at our roses and our rhubarb.

In the suburbs we are interested in little things. Each year is punctuated by the same recurring events as the year that went before—the coming of the flowers in their seasons, spring-cleaning, the sales, the buying of new garments, the visits of friends, a little gardening, a little play-going, a little holiday-making. Life for us is very ordinary.

But the city of our love is far otherwise. As to a lover the inspiration of his lady is ever present, though he may fail to realize that it is so, so to us, actively engaged in the duties of our daily round, our romantic setting is, it may be sub-consciously, an unceasing cause for self-congratulation. Life gains a greater zest when its years are passed in Edinburgh!

And, having loved her, can we ever bear to let her go?

J. M. S.

Edinburgh, 1930.

I

"MINE OWN ROMANTIC TOWN"

THE STREET OF STREETS

To us who live in Edinburgh, no less than to the visitor, Princes Street is always the centre of affairs. One may dwell at the Braids or at Liberton, at Gorgie or at Goldenacre, but one's first thought, if one is a woman, outside of one's own home, is given to the street of streets!

One may have been absent from the city of one's love, or imprisoned in the house through illness or the spring-cleaning, and one's first outing, when free to stretch one's wings, will be to see how the famous street has fared during the enforced absence. One is never too young to be without knowledge of it—witness the promenade of prams! Nor can one ever be too old, so it seems to me, to find some personal interest in its beauty.

And the secret of that allure? It cannot be entirely summed up by the cynically-inclined as " The Shops! " Not that a feminine tongue would ever seek to disparage their delights. But there is more to it than that—much more! Its natural beauty, the wonder of its Castle mounted high on the lofty rock, the green beauty of the slopes of its gardens, its associations with the great ones of the past—Scott, De Quincey, Carlyle, Stevenson, the sunshine of it, the openness. When the shop-side is speaking of the present, the gardens-side seeks surely by its climbing Castle and its dreaming spires to lift our thoughts above the fuss and fret of daily trials.

Upon these heights, in the loftiest place available, the old Castle has gathered to itself in recent years the Scottish War Memorial of which the fame is already widespread, and to which is ever climbing a countless multitude of those who have not forgotten. It is well to climb with them now and then to share for a few minutes in that wonderful atmosphere of peace and beauty, to mingle with them as, very reverently, they enter. Talking to each other in subdued tones, they wander slowly round until they reach the bay that is their own particular Holy of Holies, and pause to turn over the leaves of the book of names until their eyes tell you that they have found his that they sought. Then, in the silence, the dead come very near. . . .

It has its own panorama of the seasons, this so famous street. The young spring sun is ever eager to try his new rays upon Princes Street—it seems entirely fitting that the fairest should be the first to be honoured. The North Bridge, a thoroughfare of busyness and bustle, solid and virile and practical, seems to fare well enough without any flattery from Mr. Sol. But Princes Street, most feminine of streets, is a finished coquette, ever eager and ready to respond to his attentions.

The plots in the Gardens are not slow to take up the message of spring and to trumpet it forth through the voice of the crocuses and the daffodils, and the stiffly-upholstered hyacinths, vari-coloured, tightly packed into the corner near Sir Walter, enthroned in stone. And

wherefore should My Lady, the flowers having clothed
themselves anew, deny herself the benison of a new spring
hat? The shops, rivals in methods of subtle attraction,
will conspire to overcome any possible suggestion of hesi-
tation on her part!

And summer? Isn't summer Princes Street's most
magic time of all? Edinburgh is so wonderful in May
and June! It seems extraordinary that many of her inhabitants should flutter away as this season approaches,
when the trees begin, new-robed in their fresh green
gowns, to flirt their airy drapery in the breeze, and the
filmy blue mists creep about beneath their outspreading
branches in the Gardens, and the old Castle grows less
austere under the brightness of the summer sky, and the
flower beds burst into a glory of azaleas and hydrangeas!
Then do the chairs come out on the balconies—if we do
not possess street cafés with chairs on the pavement,
surely we possess the " next best thing " in these tea-shop
balconies, lifted up above the moving life of the street.
The panorama outspread before the tea-drinkers is one
that might well appear to be fairyland, did we not know
it to be—Edinburgh!

Following upon Assembly-time when the ministers
and their ladies descend upon us, the tourist season brings
a flood of Americans and Colonials to fill the streets, to
surge into the restaurants, to crowd around St. Giles', and
drive in char-a-bancs to the Forth Bridge and Dryburgh.
Then do the shop windows fill themselves with Scottish
souvenirs, tartan rugs and purses, pocket editions of *The
Lady of the Lake* and *The Cotter's Saturday Night,* pebble

brooches, shortbread—which shall they choose to carry back to Minnesota or Connecticut? Then do the boys, who on International days busy themselves with the sale of the rose and the thistle or the vegetable of Wales, take up and unweariedly repeat the slogan, " White heather—good luck! "

At Christmas-time Princes Street makes a potent appeal when the electric standards and the shops are glittering with a fairylike array of lights, while across the separating gulf of the gardens the lights of the Old Town twinkle forth in response to their challenge. The shimmering Christmas-tree or the beckoning hand of Father Christmas points the way to the bazaar that is the Paradise of the children. Then when the lengthy shopping-list has been worked off, when Aunt Jane's likes have been remembered and Cousin Freda's preferences not forgotten, the call of the tea-rooms becomes most irresistible, and the shoppers relax, allowing their tongues full play, over the teacups.

And what city, not excluding Paris and its *patisseries,* possesses tearooms with cakes such as Edinburgh can offer? As you sit, sipping your tea, nibbling your chocolate biscuit, you watch the old Castle being slowly drawn under the cloak of night, while the little lights, the street-lamps of Edinburgh, so dear to Robert Louis Stevenson, brighten with a suggestion of seductive intimacy.

We who " belong " have our moments, ever and anon recurring, when the beauty of the inheritance that is ours startles us afresh. Such moments come stealing upon us unawares. Immersed in affairs, intrigued with a tussle over this problem or that, we are suddenly startled by the wonderful decisive outline of the Old Town against a clear evening sky, or by the purple shadows that creep about the Castle rock, transforming it utterly.

And with all the beauty the street of streets is inseparably linked up!

SKATING ON BLACKFORD POND

RECENTLY we have experienced days when even Edinburgh lost her allure, so cold were they and bleak. Days when the flower shops held out little candles to melt the frost on their window-panes, seeking to protect their fragile contents a little, while the snowdrops and the violets must have shivered, regretting that they had ever entered a world so cruelly unkind. Days, these, when we were glad to find ourselves indoors, though even there we could scarcely keep warm. Every extra quilt and hot water bottle requisitioned for our beds—and still we shivered.

It availed little that Mr. John Frost, while he put out the street lamps that were wont to twinkle in through the window, yet drew fairy tale pictures on the selfsame panes —we really were far too cold to admire his efforts at artistic handicraft as they deserved to be admired. "It will snow to-morrow," we said, drawing our chairs closer to the blaze, trying to drive away dismal thoughts, despite the opinion of the doctor that the cold would not bring back a second visitation of the 'flu, and the more definite announcement of a nurse friend that it would drive it away instead. And the flames danced right merrily on our heaped-up fires, but, oh, dear, they needed such a lot of tending!

Then came Sunday, which justified its name, the sun drawing us out into a brighter world. The large houses of the select suburbs still retained their attitude of after-lunch somnolence. It would take more even than Mr. Frost's efforts to rouse *them* up! There are gardens overlooking Blackford Hill that, in summer, become veritable dreams of beauty—one of them is a perfect fairyland of blue forget-me-nots; they also slept. The snow had given a thin sugar coating to the shrubs in the public garden. Its seats were deserted—quite.

From the pond, however, came the sound of many voices. While others might sit at home, some to sleep, the more nervous to keep vigil over frozen taps, anticipating the great flood, young Edinburgh made the most of its opportunities on the ice. Young male Edinburgh, I should say, few of the extra 30,000 of the other sex being in evidence there at the time of my visit.

Occasionally, however, a family of humans would replace that of the swans and cygnets, father, mother, and children enjoying the unusual experience of promenading on the ice. Theirs was the less exuberant part. Long slides had been formed by the edge of the pond where schoolboys slid in close formation, so that if one had a mishap and fell he soon had a human mass on top of him. Young men joined them, conspicuous among them one who suggested the young-man-about-town type, of immaculate toilette, complete with walking-stick, and who proceeded to enjoy the fun as much as the youngest of the schoolboys.

The skaters disported themselves gracefully. One

wondered at their confidence until one recalled that they had probably been in practice at the ice-rink, so few opportunities do we have of donning our skates that the art of the ice might well become lost. People of all ages, warmly wrapped up, looked with great interest on the scene of harmless enjoyment, while the hill raised its snow-covered banks to flank it.

The birds of the pond had settled down to their restricted quarters, roped off at one end, where the ice had been broken for them. They did not seem to be particularly perturbed at thus finding themselves in reduced circumstances, and showed no inclination to venture among the humans who had usurped their rightful territory. Swans and ducks disported and preened themselves in the little water that they had, friendly hands having spread the ice with a more generous sprinkling of crumbs than usual.

And—yes, it was not mere imagination—it was certainly warmer as one walked beneath the lofty banks than one had experienced elsewhere. The scene presented at the Braid Bridge, in the wood where autumn lingers long, was a striking one. The wood was still carpeted thick with the brown leaves of the toilette that My Lady Autumn had discarded, but through among them, under ice and snow, flowed the stream, snow-white against the brown, the water showing only where breakages had occurred in the ice.

Recognizing among these so graceful skaters personal friends who are known to excel in many other walks of life but whose skating prowess was undreamt of till now, one began to ponder their versatility. How do they find time for so many interests? There are people who can achieve the seeming impossible, without having any dalliance with the old problem—shall we squander our energies over a variety of interests or conserve them, with the utmost concentration, for one particular pursuit, or two?

Some people there are who appear to do everything well. They excel at work and at play. There are others so much afraid of distracting their attention from the one thing they want to do, be it music or jam-making, or anything else, that they refuse to have their interest directed into any side-tracks. Apart from necessary exercise— even, perhaps, at the sacrifice of that—their whole attention must be given to it, with the dream, may be, that some notable *magnum opus* shall one day astonish the world.

While some concentration—a good deal, in fact—is absolutely necessary, no achievement, linked up with humanity, was ever gained by separating ourselves from our fellow-beings. Haven't we all known the type of student who, devoted to his or her books and shut off from all other interests, has fossilised long before even the age of thirty!

On the other hand, we have known those of brilliant promise, who have spent themselves in a variety of directions, and in the end achieved less than nothing! It is a matter, I suppose, that each of us must settle for ourselves, drinking our red wine or white as the case may be, to the dregs. And surely, if in the end dissatisfaction crowns our efforts, our own conscience will prick us sufficiently, without other people reminding us " If you had done so and so——! "

But I have wandered far from that company of merry skaters! I can only plead the cold as an excuse for having digressed thus into the more serious strain!

VISITING-HOUR AT THE ROYAL INFIRMARY

THERE are other queues in Edinburgh than those that wait for theatre or cinema. There is one that, starting at the Infirmary gate, stretches, most afternoons, right down the Meadow Walk. On Saturdays and Sundays, when the husbands and fathers are able to join it, it is longer than ever.

It is composed of widely dissociated units, this queue. The prosperous-looking woman, attired in a fur coat and a bright new spring hat, may, and does, rub shoulders with the woman of the slums, wrapt in a huge black shawl, her head unprotected. The fur-coated dame carries a neat little package and a spray of daffodils carefully wrapped round with tissue paper. The beshawled one also has a package, bulkier indeed, but having the secret of its contents less carefully concealed.

While the one lady is accompanied by a little girl immaculately attired in a neat brown fur-trimmed coat and straw hat with school badge in front, the other has a smaller child, scarcely more than a baby, her light yellow hair unhampered, like her mother's, by any covering, clad in a bunchy frock of blue cotton, and wrapped round with a bright magenta-coloured " woollie."

While street-musicians of diverse sorts do their best to beguile the tedium of waiting for the theatre queue, the

VISITING-HOUR AT THE ROYAL INFIRMARY

Infirmary queue is the haunt of the flower-sellers. They may lack the picturesqueness of London flower-girls or the Parisian *merchandes des quatre saisons,* but, financially, they may be in a better position, for their flowers are very much in demand. Their baskets, just at present, are heavily laden with daffodils, narcissi, and tulips— but, chiefly, daffodils. From these baskets comes much of that golden radiance that lightens up the long wards of the Infirmary.

The bare-headed woman, who draws her shawl tightly round her to keep out the cold, refuses to be outdone either in the multitude or in the magnitude of her offerings by her richer neighbours of the queue. Giving some pennies to the tiny mite who accompanies her, she points her finger in the direction of the flower-seller. The baby steps out and stands before him, expectant but silent. As she is unable to make known her demands, he makes a selection for her from his flowers; her tiny hand can scarcely hold them all, so that a pink and white tulip slips out just as she regains her place beside her mother.

The queue of well-clad and scantily-clad, town people and country people, all equally laden with parcels and daffodils, begins to move very slowly. As it nears the gate some units who have newly arrived seek to become, without the boredom of waiting, an integral part of the queue. Their intentions are frustrated by an alert policeman. Presently, however, he proceeds to challenge some others who have won their place and held it quite legitimately, receiving a sharp retort and reprimand at so unworthy an accusation.

26

VISITING-HOUR AT THE ROYAL INFIRMARY

Passing inside the gates, the queue distributes itself throughout the different blocks, along the various corridors. Some visitors traverse the long corridor to the very end in search of the ward they want. Reaching it, again they distribute themselves round the different beds. So immaculate is the ward with its white beds, its highly-polished floor, its flower-vases observing just proportions in their distance from each other, that it is impossible for the casual visitor to imagine its equanimity upset.

The patients, cheered by the sight of their friends, are perhaps on their best behaviour. Here and there one is saddened, indeed, by the sight of a figure lying silent—the operation day too near as yet to admit of visitors, but, for the most part, they are wonderfully cheerful, those others who have passed the crisis. At the door stands the trim, white-aproned nurse, keeping an eagle, but a sympathetic, eye on all that goes on. Two visitors only are permitted at a bed at a time. The intrusion of a third, with the best intentions in the world—probably hugging to himself the maxim of " the more the merrier! "—is a signal for her kindly, but decisive, intervention.

At the beds it would seem very probable that exactly the same questions are being asked, the answers, perhaps scarcely more varied, but individually so interesting, given. The gifts are distributed. Apart from offerings of eggs and fruit, it is a case of daffodils—nearly all the way! Someone has brought a hydrangea in a pot. It rears itself proudly as if conscious of the consolation stored up in the beautiful blue flower which it is bringing into the midst of suffering. On one bed lies a young woman.

Her operation is to take place next day. Her husband has brought the baby in a blue coat—and a bottle of milk to keep it happy! She is fondling it tenderly. When the ominous bell sounds for the withdrawal of the visitors, she kisses it greedily; her husband, in turn, kisses her— perhaps for the last time, Mary Rose would suggest—and goes off, carrying the baby. Her eyes follow them to the door of the ward. It is a sad farewell. But the operation successfully over, she is soon sitting up, bright-eyed, entertaining her visitors.

Each patient assumes for his neighbours an interest and importance that, with other distractions, he would scarcely possess. The " cases," even in a single ward, present an amazing variety. About a young girl from the far north with a septic hand there is a note of pathetic uncertainty. Another has undergone a critical operation, and the verdict is the disquieting one—" Not yet out of danger." Others are already safely on the road to recovery.

Perhaps an infirmary ward is the last place in the world where one would expect to find humour. And yet there is quite a generous sprinkling of this salutary ingredient, judging from little stories that one hears from the patients themselves. The slightest little happening becomes noteworthy as varying that monotonous routine which nibbles up the slow-passing days and nights. There is, for example, the woman who, admitted for some other ailment, turned sick one day, and explains that, to her quite unjustifiably, she was " put through an operation for appendicitis! " She fails to share the enthusiasm of the doctor at the prompt measures taken to eradicate future trouble! A young girl, supposed—according to the unreliable evidence of another patient!—to be threatened with the same affliction, was inclined to treat her appearance there as a joke, and subsequently owned up to having consumed at a sitting two tins of caramels!— quite sufficient to occasion the discomfort experienced!

Sometimes those sitting at the beds near the door and in view of the door of the operating theatre are fated to get a little silent insight into the smooth working of the institution. To the uninitiated an operation is a fearsome proceeding, wrapt round with terror, dismay, abandonment to despair, and a general all-round lack of control! Then, perhaps on a quiet Sunday afternoon, suddenly one of these same uninitiated (and essentially morbidminded!) perceives the appearance of white-coated attendants in the vicinity of the theatre; a trolley is silently wheeled out, reappearing again bearing a silent figure upon it. The door closes.

A short time intervenes, and, again silently, the trolley emerges, and somewhere in a neighbouring ward the silent figure is restored to his bed. The sound of running water is heard in the theatre, where the nurse is seen passing in and out. Such an episode arouses much sympathetic interest in the patients who have themselves successfully passed through the same ordeal.

The bell rings, and the good-byes are said. The waiting nurse is ready to smile in token of sympathy. The invasion of visitors was, for the most part, and save for the footfalls in the corridors, a silent one. Silent, too, they steal away. Some who came with disquieting fears have had these laid to rest; others, perhaps, have had their fears increased. Trickling out of the various doors, the stream of departing visitors swells to a flood ere it reaches the gate. Other friends are waiting there, who, not having the necessary admission cards, are eager for information of the sick ones. Then, very quickly, they are all absorbed into the daily rush of the city.

Meanwhile it is tea-time in the wards. The eggs which the nurse has previously collected from the patients, identifying each with the name of its owner, come back boiled, and accompanied by tea and toast, to tempt the appetite that is not yet outrageously robust.

IN A PENTLANDS RETREAT

THE Calf Girl lives, with her collie dog, at the bottom of steep Caerketton. Her cottage has left the farm-steading behind at a short distance, though it keeps watching her all the time. That little wooden shack of hers, with its staunch bodyguard of trees, clings tenaciously to the hillside. At the side of the cottage a slow-flowing burn makes continuous music. Sometimes it is with a feeble attempt at mimic tumult that it roars in the Calf Girl's ears of a winter's night.

The Calf Girl rises early in the morning to attend to the needs of the little animals whose experimental feeding is her special care—about the time when the ploughmen are leading out their " pairs," and the implements are being trundled off to the distant fields. Nell, the Calf Dog, assists, sometimes merely under a French interpretation of the word, at the feeding of the calves, at the dosing of them with cod liver oil—a remedy for many ills in the world of calves—at the weekly weighing of them, according to the best principles of Calf Welfare.

The cottage and its garden are shut off by a fence from the encircling field. Round her garden, early in summer, the Calf Girl planted pansies and dahlias, antirrhinums and chrysanthemums, that a flutter of colour might gladden her eyes when she opened her cottage door in the morning. When she closed it at night she dreamed that her eyes might feast on a riot of purple and red, bronze and yellow. The riot, however, was more restrained than she expected.

For the farm horses, wandering in their summer play-time about the field, stretched their long necks over her inadequate fence and nipped off a geranium head here, the stalk of a dahlia there. That treacherous act troubled the Calf Girl a little; but being of a philosophical turn of mind, she lifted her eyes to the hills, and decided that, after all, a green colour scheme leaves little to be desired.

One glorious summer day the Town Girl came to visit her. Nell recognised her in the distance and ran out to welcome her, escorting her to the door of the hut. Only to those whom she knows and trusts does Nell thus extend the cordiality of a welcome. She will bark all day should a strange angling-man appear and take up his position by the side of the burn, seeking to wheedle the unwilling fish into tasting the sweetness of his pendent worm.

The hut did not seem lonely that day. Painted bright red and green, it looked quite picturesque in the sunshine. The Town Girl compared it to an Alpine chalet. The hawthorns behind it were filling the air with perfume, and spraying the ground with a rain of snowy petals from the bridal robe they were discarding. At the shepherd's house farther up the hill the rambler roses were beginning their summer game of hide-and-seek about the fence and the trellis-work.

Through the doorway of the hut the trees waved their

green branches coquettishly, saying, " Come out and play with us." To the right dreamy eyes could fasten on haunted Woodhouselee; in front lay Roslin; to the left, unseen, the " Grey Metropolis." . . .

The Town Girl said, " Isn't it lovely? " And after that she said, " Isn't it sweet? " And then she said, " I could live here for ever! " And the Calf Girl listened, well pleased that her surroundings should be appreciated. Then she thought of the lonely nights of winter . . . the mud . . . the snow . . . the mornings when her pathway had to be dug out. And she looked at the Town Girl's patent shoes, her stockings of sheerest silk. But she said nothing.

On a bleak, cold day of spring the Town Girl came again. April had forgotten that her hands should have been filled with violets. She had neglected to collect soft breezes and sunny showers. Instead she harked back to winter. The wind was so cold that the Town Girl drew her furs closer around her, though it scarcely penetrated the Calf Girl's uniform. Determined, however, not to miss anything, she accepted an invitation to climb the lower slopes of Caerketton. Nell, of course, was ready to join the expedition. So the trio set off by the tumbling burn, where it fell among the trees just beginning to bud, the hawthorns that had not yet foreseen the need to prepare bridal attire. The shepherd had closed his door against the menace of the night. The birds had forgotten how to sing.

They came to the dipping-place, full of unpleasant significance for Nell, who, twice a year, undergoes the

33   c

ordeal by water—and sheep-dip! While the Calf Girl paused to explain its mysteries to the Town Girl, who, unlike Nell, had never seen such a place before, Nell, seeking to distract attention from the sinister pool, gave chase to some make-believe rabbit. The dipping-box safely left behind, she crept back to her mistress's heels.

The walk was muddy, in places very slippery, and the Town Girl's feet were thinly clad. But she said she enjoyed it—she loved to have her stockings and shoes bemuddied! And once again the Calf Girl heard her, not wholly convinced.

She, however, thinks neither of the mud nor the lonelines when, seated at her own fireside in her Pentlands retreat, Nell stretched at her feet, she takes up her violin and begins to draw her bow across the strings.

THIS WAY TO FAIRYLAND!

HAVE you been to Fairyland? I found myself there the
other day in a world of sunshine and colour and sweet
sounds, after I had passed under the pink hawthorns arch-
ing the entrance to the Edinburgh Botanic Gardens.
True, I did not see the fairy folk, but surely they were
hiding behind the bushes—perhaps even lurking in
these wide-open purple bells of the rhododendrons! I
could quite well imagine them smiling to each other
rather whimsically as they exchanged remarks over the
obtuseness of those mortals who think they know so
much and to whom so many secrets have yet to be re-
vealed!

Where there are fairies there are always children to be
found. The Botanic Gardens have become, in these
sunny afternoons, a replica of Kensington Gardens or the
Park Monçeau. Everywhere are perambulators, everywhere are little children, tumbling about on the grass,
playing hide and seek round this rose-bush or that
laburnum. To *them* may even be vouchsafed a glimpse
of one or other of Puck's merry crew—who knows?

Great coloured screens of rhododendrons confront one
on entering. Screens that are crimson and white and
rose, dark purple, the heliotrope that is closely related to
blue or that more nearly allied to pink! Some of the

35

bushes are just beginning to shed their petals in showers of coloured rain. A dark red bush flaunts itself beside the pond in a bold attempt to outshine the pink azalea at the opposite side, while a chorus of purple applause is raised by the primulas that cluster round the water's edge. The ducks have given over their sailing around the water-lilies, and have come to rest, all huddled together among those plants that make a little island all by themselves. Some young students stretched on the grass are, surely, engaged in the discussion of some weighty subject.

Every little while the green pathways, all sparkling in the sunlight, are brightened with the glittering gold of a laburnum tree, or the promise of a pink briar rose just struggling into bloom; the fresh fragrant appeal of lemon-coloured violas set in circle around a young larch tree, or the full-blasted triumph of a regally-dressed rhododendron bush. One need not penetrate within the hot-houses in search of colour in these June days; it is to be found in plenty in this fairyland of beauty out-of-doors—not least in those glorious clumps of azaleas!

Their colour-schemes may be less bold than those adopted by the proud rhododendrons; they disregard the latter's favourite purple tints, preferring the pink that is so uniquely their own, so fresh and inspiring, and an orange that seeks almost to rival the hue of the tiger-lily. Mixed with these they have chosen, by way of contrast, pale tints—white and cream and pink—producing wonderful colour combinations on which the eye could feast throughout a whole long summer's afternoon. How the fairies must revel in their colours, each little elf poising herself now to peep into a cream-coloured azalea heart, now into one that is, in its rose-pinkness, so radiant with *joie-de-vivre!*

That wide herbaceous-border, flanked and sheltered by the great hedge, will be loved particularly, I think, by the older people, with their memories of the country gardens of their long-ago. To them even the colourful azaleas may suggest something that is a little " new-fangled." But their eyes will brighten as they alight on one after another of the old favourites; a graceful columbine, a sturdy lupin, indigo-blue; pale violas and brown pansy-faces, geums, veronica, campanulas, or a wide-spreading briar-rose.

In that same border there stands a laburnum that would have startled me had I not seen one that presented a similar phenomenon in a manse-garden in Peeblesshire but two days previously. The drooping tassels of this laburnum are of two colours, the familiar yellow being mixed with pink! It is produced, I am informed, by the grafting of cytisus with a laburnum, the flowers of the cytisus turning into laburnum tassels rather smaller than those that are yellow. The Peeblesshire laburnum, I was interested to learn, usually had three colours—yellow, pink, and purple. It is known as Adam's tree. If some day one chances upon the tree that will be known as Eve's, one is willing to believe that she, with her feminine love of colour, will have introduced an even wider range of hues!

In the course of my Fairyland peregrinations, I found

myself ushered in by romantic flower ways that hint at the wonder to which they lead, to the rock garden. Clumps of creamy flowers and tall blue spikes of blossoms that might have been made of paper guarded my own entrance to the particular place of enchantment. The aubrietia that everywhere has carpeted the rocks with purple, is fading now, but masses of glowing helianthe-mums supply a brilliancy of salmon-pink and red and yellow. Can't you see the elves and gnomes having a hilarious time o' nights tumbling about these rocky steps and about the pond where the murmur of running water adds its pleasant note to the perfumed air? Rock-roses and yellow alyssum, forget-me-nots and pale heliotrope asters—they will not so much as turn a leaf even if the merry crew indulge in the maddest of helter-skelters this way and that, all over and around them!

Behind a slab of rock I caught a glimpse of the tiniest, blackest viola I have ever seen. I can imagine an inquir-ing elf pausing wonderingly before it of a summery June night, seeking to read the mystery of its inscrutable yellow eyes!

Around the wall of the rock-garden all kinds of fasci-nating plants are hanging out their colourful heads as though beseeching the botanists who wander by to read their uninspiring Latin names—but our time is too short for any such somewhat doubtful indulgence. Let us fol-low this narrow pathway instead which is guarded by the rhododendron that is heliotrope and the rhododen-dron whose big bell-flowers are white. Let us leave the paths altogether and feel the soft, velvety grass carpet beneath our feet and wander in search of the lilacs and laburnums that he or she who keeps strictly to the beaten track never sees. Let us rest for a little to inhale the scented breath of the Gardens, while a chorus of bird-music fills our ears, and our eyes can feast themselves unendingly and without surfeit on a mass of glowing colour!

And, of course, you would like to wander with me up to the terrace? I am not sure that the fairies come there so often: there are fewer "hidey-holes," and I scarcely think they would care to utilize instead these fresh orange-painted waste-paper baskets! But we can afford to neglect the "little folk" just for a few minutes while we gaze over our own romantic town, that looms like a veritable city of fairyland itself through the blue mists. Beyond the quiet green ways of the Gardens, the flaming bushes, the bird-music—this dim city of mystery, quiescent, silent! Above the mass of huddled buildings rise the great land-marks, its palaces and towers, its churches. Misty against the sky-line is the ever-dominating outline of the Castle, and further off still, much fainter, the climbing, peak-marked line of the Pentlands.

As we walk through the fairyland of the Gardens to where the pink hawthorns flank the way to the tram-line which leads to the heart of the city of allure, surely we cannot but breathe a little prayer of thankfulness because to us is vouchsafed so much more than a Pisgah-view thereof!

A RAMBLE DOWN THE CANONGATE

WILL you come for a ramble with me down the Canongate? Let me warn you beforehand that you, a stranger, will require to keep bolstering up your spirits all the time with the thought of the glories that these ancient walls have known in the past, lest you become overwhelmed by the squalor of the unsavoury closes and their unwashed inhabitants!

We who live in Edinburgh are apt, in our journeyings up and down the old Canongate, to pass these historic buildings with the most casual of glances, forgetful of their memories. To-day we shall pause to note the elaborate coats-of-arms over grimy doorways which once opened on homes whose aristocratic inhabitants shared in Royal favour at Holyrood. Their windows still, at intervals, look out upon the passing of the King and Queen, or a Prince or Princess of the Royal House. You will do well to remember these things—such thoughts will divert your attention from the sordidness and the grime!

Unaccustomed eyes are always impressed by the displays of washing hung from rows of windows high up on the lofty tenements or " lands ", the variously-assorted garments boldly fluttering in the public gaze—*we* pass them by unnoticed!

There are four main classes of shops that keep recur-

ring with considerable insistence as we traverse the
" Royal Mile " : the butchers' shops whose crowded contents are crudely displayed; those which hold up rows and
more rows of memorial wreaths composed of artificial
flowers; pawnshops whose windows are heaped with
dusty piles of cast-off clothing, waiting apparently until
they moulder out of existence; and shops or houses of
alcoholic refreshment round the doors of which men sit,
expectantly waiting. Antique shops, too, have their own
part to play in this old-world street, displaying the
trinket-boxes and miniatures, the necklaces and rings that
were once gifted with kisses and tenderly treasured, but
that are now patiently waiting until the connoisseur
comes along to make an unsentimental purchase. You
will also, no doubt, be interested to observe that, on this
hot summer's day the Canongate baker sees fit to announce on a card that he is ready to supply Fresh Straw-
berry Tarts!

In a progress of the Royal Mile much of the tale of sad
humanity lies open before us if we choose to read it. No
matter how stiflingly hot the day, practically every woman
in the Canongate seeks to cover up toilette deficiencies
—nor can one wonder at her—by wrapping herself
round with a large, dark shawl. The shawl usually
shelters a child as well. These women wait too—but
without expectation. They wander about the pavements,
they sit gossiping round the entries, doing nothing at all
—hands are so often idle down there—punctuating their
conversation occasionally with a sharp word to an erring
child. They are bare-headed for the most part, their hair

twisted up untidily; on many of their faces life's experience has written a look of hardness. Sometimes you
meet one of the older women who walks with downcast
eyes which, you realise, must contain a world of sadness.
Yet age matters little down there: that enveloping shawl
is a great leveller of the generations.

When we peep within the courts and wynds we
realise, even more forcefully, the squalor of it all—and
that despite a praiseworthy attempt to whitewash the old
wooden beams. Many of the courts reach a premature
conclusion in a high gateway as a barrier beyond which
all else is mystery. Others, however, are much more
spacious. One of the richest in its treasure-trove of
memories is Bakehouse Close—shall we peep within?
We penetrate to it through the " pend " that passes beneath the old town house of the Marquis of Huntly, still
turning a timbered front upon the street and bearing
inscriptions in Latin. Here, as elsewhere, whitewash is
conspicuous. A few yards within we find, in a tiny square
on the left, the former residence of one Acheson of Gosford, which, upon one occasion, Lady Jane Grey honoured
with her presence for nine nights. Beneath the old door-
day, bearing still the Gosford arms and the date 1633 there
passes a workman on his way home for his mid-day meal,
climbing by the old winding wooden stair to his own
particular niche in the historic mansion now distinguished
by window panes that are broken and grimy.

Huntly House secures a peep at the Calton Hill and
the Royal High School across the green slopes of the old
Canongate Churchyard, where lie buried many famous

men, among them Robert Fergusson the poet, and at least one famous woman—Burns's Clarinda.

Dunbar's Close too has a share in the wonderful prospect—perhaps by way of compensation for having the graveyard directly in front of its houses, their lower windows being darkened by the more ambitious memorials that even surmount the high wall—an unfair croachment, this, of the dead upon the rights of the living!

Passing Moray House and Queensberry House, each trailing long annals of history behind it, you will find your nostrils assailed by the heavy aroma of the breweries, and I think you will be glad to escape for a little within the privacies of the Palace of Holyroodhouse. The stranger will notice sooner than the native the curiously-gabled houses on the left known as the Abbey Strand. They have wandered out of their age and generation, and suffer for the transgression by having their doors and windows securely locked and barred.

There is an air of haunting sadness brooding over the Palace of Mary Stuart to-day. It was not so but a few weeks ago when the grassy space in the quadrangle was occupied by red-coated bandsmen, and music played, arousing Holyrood from its slumber; when daintily dressed ladies and men in black coats or in bright uniform assembled to honour the Lord High Commissioner. Now the revel is over, and the Palace has sunk again into that sleep from which even the summer visitors fail to arouse it. To-day one wanders in solitude through the Chapel Royal, roofless to the sky, to peep through the closed gateway at the summer beauty of the gardens,

A RAMBLE DOWN THE CANONGATE

only a few weeks past the scene of a gay Garden Party.

Deserted too are the historic rooms. One gazes on the mouldering finery of Mary's bed, and dreams a little over the work-box, remembering how, centuries ago, its lid was opened and closed by her white fingers alone. Through this very window she watched, perhaps not a little sadly, the town that was encroaching so close upon her Palace gates. Through that other window we see the same hills that Mary was wont to gaze upon, for whatever else is changed, Arthur's Seat and the Crags remain unaltered.

In a rush of remembrance, one's thoughts turn to the ghosts of Holyrood, the shades of Darnley and Rizzio and the rest, who steal about these rooms unseen when the visitors have gone and darkness has re-claimed them for its own. It is a place to brood in, indeed, there where the ghosts hold high carnival o' nights. Do they enact again the murder of Rizzio, I wonder? Does John Knox still hover around intent upon making a Protestant of Mary? And does the Queen still weepingly refuse to be won over?

But a party of school-children with clattering feet appear, accompanied by a guide, and the ghosts who might have been tempted to linger to interrupt my solitude retire again to the shades. And youth with a casual eye, passes by the pink satin chair, gold-embroidered, that is treasured within its glass case, and gives but a fleeting glance at the tiny oratory where Mary Queen of Scots was wont to breathe her evening prayers.

44

A RAMBLE DOWN THE CANONGATE

Who shall answer the questions of the silences? . . .
One seeks the Canongate again, and passes within the
old Whitehorse Close, less grey than the rest when the sun
shines on its red roofs and green painted window-sills,—
this Close where Prince Charlie lodged. This is washing-
day in the Canongate, and the rite of the tub has been
celebrated not least extensively in the old Whitehorse
Close—witness the garments that flutter from its windows, that long string of drying clothes that stretches
from wall to wall right across the Close! The women as
usual stand about and gossip—and wait. Some tiny
children, caring not even to play, stand idly by. A
canary gaily trills his song in a cage hung over the lintel
of a one-time famous door.

Near by are some of these dark little cupboards of
shops, which one enters by descending a few steps to peer
furtively as into a cave. That they are places of mystery
is further emphasised by the heaped-up, dusty condition
of their contents.

A brighter note is contributed by the wooden toys that
adorn the windows of Lady Haig's Poppy Factory, which
signifies a real effort to help those in urgent need. On
a grey November day its scarlet poppies of remembrance
add a glorious gleam of colour to the old Canongate.
Reid's Court with its progressive nursery school marks
another stage in a constructive direction.

We pass presently almost under the eaves of John
Knox's House which juts out picturesquely into the
High Street. Its windows are crowded with souvenirs,
with tartan goods, with copies of the works of Burns and

Scott. Adjoining it is the old curiosity shop to which Queen Mary is a frequent visitor whenever she visits the Scottish metropolis.

The street, as it draws nearer the North Bridge, begins to take on some semblance of the character of that busier thoroughfare. It widens out, grows breezier; its shops are larger, more up-to-date. Emerging on the North Bridge, we realise suddenly that the people too have changed, their appearance being no longer unkempt, un-cared-for.

But perhaps their outstanding point of difference is that, unlike the people of the Canongate, they hurry and bustle about, they scramble and rush, having no time to stand about—and wait!

THE ROAD ROUND THE HILLS

THE other day I journeyed by " the road round the hills."
Not on foot, as is the way of the true pilgrim; these days
employ a means of transit less romantic. Perchance when
another hundred years have rolled away, the motor car
may have become a vehicle as much preferred by the
artist as is the old-fashioned stage coach as a subject for
his brush.

Away, then, by Hunter's Tryst, and Dreghorn, and
picturesque Colinton, with its bridge opening up such
charming prospects; catching here a glint of autumn's
warning note of gold in the trees, there a flash of scarlet
from a rowan-laden tree. On, past fields of yellowing
corn just opened up for the reapers, and others where the
stooks already stand all glittering gold, past gardens
giving pink peeps at standard ramblers, and trellises lost
sight of under their burden of roses.

So we came to Balerno. And of the main streets of
Balerno I should like to say something nice, even flatter-
ing, but my truthful pen shrinks from the act. Balerno
may flatter itself on the music of its name, the beauty of
its surroundings, but never upon the picturesque quali-
ties of its central thoroughfare! Moreover, the smell of
the paper mills repels, rather than encourages attention.

Balerno provides, however, a delightful place for tea,

in a little bungalow that has secured an exclusive view of the Black Hill. Its front garden is a veritable riot of colour. True, we missed the golden glory of that hedge of broom, but roses, pink and crimson, were still opening wide their petalled hearts, tall monkshood was impressing its note of purple-blue, montbretia was just revealing its flame-coloured petals, and a tall phlox wore blossoms of rich shell pink. Rock roses bordered the crazy paths, and a curious kind of clover with variegated leaves hovered about the doorstep, offering itself humbly as a carpet for the feet that go out of their way to avoid crushing it.

Inside, you may sit in the hall or in the charming room that leads from it. The windows are curtained with pink; the tables are covered with blue. Roses, pink and heliotrope, fill a floating bowl on the centre of the table, and are repeated in festoons on the tea-cups. Dainty water-colours look down from the walls, and the bookcases hold—just all the books that one loves best! The sandwiches, the home-made scones and cakes, are deliciously appetising. But I am in need of reminding myself that I did not set out to write about a tea-place, however glorified, but about a road!

Turning about, and leaving Balerno behind, we passed into the loneliness of the road leading to the Lang Whang—through lanes of shadowy trees, past fields of yellow corn, and thence on to the open moorland. It is possible that the road might not win your heart captive just at once. It has its memories of Roman legionaries and Border thieves, and long and lonely journeys at midnight in mid-winter. But the ghosts of the past may be slow to exert their fascinating power.

To the right Kaimes Hill and Dalmahoy Hill make a feeble attempt at maintaining that lofty appearance with which we have grown familiar from looking towards them from the Braids; they seem to have shrunk into comparative insignificance. The Cairn Hills appear on the left, as we spin past Böll of Bere, a lonely white-washed farmhouse which makes little attempt at attracting attention to itself.

Another house, a little further on, seeks to placate the passer-by with its offer of new-laid eggs. Then there comes into a view a roofless cottage—so many derelict walls are seen out by the Lang Whang—which, to our amusement, a horse has found most accommodating as an improvised stable. He stands inside, satisfied and at peace, reaching almost as high as the walls.

It is from the lonely house of Little Vantage that the road is known as the Lang Whang, a twisting, winding road, avoiding streamlets, crossing bridges, passing farms, and sometimes taking a long stretch with little untoward to remark upon, save the loneliness of it all. The walls of the unpretentious Little Vantage, once a toll house and white-washed are now smeared and storm-stained. The house has been introduced by John Buchan into one of his novels. Nearby there leads the path to the Cauldstaneslap which holds an old drove road pressed tight between the two Cairn hills, and through which, in the "good old days," many a convoy of

Border thieves advanced to harry the fertile lands of Lothian.

On our left appears Harper Rig reservoir, presenting a strained and dried-up appearance and still despite the recent August floods, drained of about half of its water.

It is lightsome, occasionally, to desert the highway, and wander down the byway. We did so here for a closer view of Cairns Castle, which, close pressed beside its companion modern dwelling, guards the reservoir.

The ruined castle had little to offer, save its memories. It was built five hundred years ago, as the guardian of the road through the hills. Originally there were two towers, but within the last seventy years one has disappeared, and the remaining tower is fast crumbling to decay, a split almost cleaving it in twain. It makes little attempt to remind us of a glorious past; its dungeons and cellars are hidden away; only the upper parts of its walls look out above the encircling greenery, while a rowan bush, occupying a vantage point on the top of the walls, brings new life to the dead. Even the reservoir has crept away this summer; its stony surrounding rim encircles a tract of dry land such as might have appeared when the waters of the Red Sea withdrew.

Contrasting with the grey walls of the old castle suggestive only of decay, rises its modern white-washed neighbour, a house built in 1872, content also to look out on the loneliness. It possesses a smooth lawn and a flower-border gay with monkshood and delphiniums beside the wall which at other times shuts off the reservoir.

Even the boat that, whilom, plied the waters of the

reservoir, lay upturned on dry land. A young game-keeper, his bag on his back, had sole possession of the narrow winding road by which we rejoined the highway.

Thence, we sped by the lonely windings of the Lang Whang, through the moorland over which the heather has spread its purple carpet. Here and there a car had paused that its occupants might gather a souvenir. Occasionally a new wooden fence makes an attempt at bordering the road, but soon desists, leaving it to its own devices. Some anglers were busy whipping a tiny streamlet, whether with zest or boredom one had not time to decide.

A peep at Carnwath's unpretentious street, another at Newbigging with its fine old market cross, then on to Dunsyre, so delightfully situated, with its Covenanting memories, and its houses peering this way and that. Dolphinton, the next village, with its curious monument-crowned " Kippit Hill " and its scattered houses, whose wooden porches form a distinctive feature of the local architecture, is also very attractive. Thence, homeward by West Linton and Carlops and Hillend.

I should like to have inserted some poetical allusions to the sun playing with colour on moorland and heather, but Mr. Sol was disobliging and refused to peep out of a dull and thundery sky, which was rather depressing. That long stretch of hill-encircling road, with the sun lighting it up, that would be wonderful indeed!

THE UNCHANGING HILLS

EVENING—on " the furzy hills of Braid "!

We are fortunate indeed in the surroundings that lie about our very doors, associated so intimately with two such literary giants as Sir Walter Scott and Robert Louis Stevenson. The Braids—Sir Walter dreamed away his boyhood's days among them, browsing over tales of old romance, while the city lay stretched beneath him. The Pentlands—who thinks of his " hills of home " without remembering R. L. S. whose Swanston retreat lies over yonder, snugly gathered in under Caerketton's protecting crags?

It is ours to gaze upon that same panorama which delighted the " Wizard's " eyes in years gone by—the panorama of the unchanging hills. From the wooded Craiglockhart Hills the vista stretches past Corstorphine Hill with its lofty tower, over that wide area of silent roofs picked out with spires, until the platform of the Salisbury Crags rears itself arrestingly and the dark blue summit of Arthur's Seat peers round the shoulder of Blackford Hill. Those who have been privileged to view the city from the air tell us that its green spaces never before seemed so impressive or so widespread. Here, in the forefront of our picture, a wealth of greenery contrasts refreshingly with the red roofs of the new houses. Beyond the city, now wreathed in soft smoke-clouds, extends its wide frame of summer-blue sea. Farther round there is Craigmillar Castle rising aloft to break the sky-line, and across another stretch of sea, North Berwick Law and the Bass appear, indomitable and staunch. . . . A satisfying prospect indeed!

Very peaceful it is here, the golfers out of sight and forgotten. Only the cawing of rooks, the bleating of distant sheep, the clatter of the milk-cans at the farm across the road to break the silence. The city too looks perfectly serene. We know that it possesses squalid slums where wretched women hover about the entries; we know that it contains hospitals and homes where suffering rages rampant. But all the squalor and pain have been blotted out of our picture; only the serenity remains.

The city may change—there are many red roofs in the picture that would seem strange to Sir Walter—but the hills remain unaltered. The generations come and go, and the hills look down complacently on each in its turn. There are children over there whose fingers gather flowers as other little fingers have plucked the daisies and the bluebells of centuries of summers. Old men of the succeeding generations have taken their daily walks round the hills, even as that old man is doing now; their wives, also of one generation, then another, have accompanied them, scarcely less feeble themselves, yet able to keep a kindly maternal eye upon them. And then they have gone away, and the hills, with heartless nonchalance, have looked down, with the same complacency on those who took their place.

Our friends, too, change with the changing years. Think of those who shared the benches with us at school, who made up our little world. Some have disappeared in this material world; some into the next. Of only a few do we know anything to-day. Nor need we grieve over-much—it is a mistake to cling too tenaciously to the interests of the past. " Earth separates as well as heaven " is the epitaph that might be written over many a promising friendship, now as dead as if the grave had closed over it. We have the satisfaction of knowing that the few remain as unchanging as the everlasting hills.

Sometimes of an evening we take the path that R. L. S. took, not so very long ago—the path that leads also hillwards, to Swanston amid these " hills of home." It winds away from the noise of the highway round by Comiston House with its cluster of richly foliaged trees, where the cawing of the rooks rings placidly in the air, interrupted at intervals by the voice of a peacock.

We wander presently through all the paraphernalia, the carts and hen-houses and implements of a farm—the farm that stares all day at the city, and at the red-roofed bungalows that stand out from the golden carpet of whins now wide outspread over the Braids.

Through a gateway, we secure a flowery peep at the gardens of Comiston House, before entering the narrow path that emerges on the road to Swanston, less lonely, less secluded now, than in Stevenson's time. And there, again, we pause, as did the psalmist of old, looking for encouragement from the everlasting hills.

THE UNCHANGING HILLS

As to us, so to those who come after us the hills will grant their aid. Nor need we envy them over-much. For we shall have passed on.

IMPRESSIONS OF A SASSENACH

To hear what strangers think about our city is interesting, often amusing, and sometimes beneficial. Of course I looked forward to what my London friend, Millicent, had to say about our grey metropolis when she came to me for her long-promised visit. Her remark when she alighted at our Braids terminus was particularly satisfactory: " Why, what wonderful air you have! I feel as if I were at the seaside! "

London has listened to Millicent's infant prattle and presided over her maidenhood's dreams. Other parts of the world, those that lie beyond the Channel, she has visited. But Scotland—never! I don't know that she ever expected to see it. I am not sure that she was not the Londoner who once asked depreciatingly, " Is there anything to *see* there? " (She would disown that remark now!) Then the unexpected happened. She took her warmest wraps with her, for cold and treacherous is the north, and she caught the train at Euston at the midnight hour.

Our grey Metropolis must have heard that she was coming, else how did it know to look its loveliest on the morning of her arrival?

When Millicent proceeded to look at the Castle, the mists creeping about its rock, and all the well-known landmarks, for the first time, I almost envied her these first impressions, which one would like well to experience over again. But to do so one would need to become a child, and emerging from the station, appear in a strange Princes Street to look in vain for the familiar buildings of the main street of the only town one knew. My own sensation, on such an occasion, was, I remember, " I shall never feel at home here! " Less overwhelming, however, must be the emotions of the child, or the woman, who steps into the street from a London background.

The tree-like appearance of the Scott Monument struck her, for out of the mists it loomed almost like a spruce, its branches tightly gathered around it—or, to put it less romantically, almost liked a closed umbrella!

The seven hills of our city soon began to make their presence felt—Millicent has not ceased to speak of them ever since she arrived. " There are hills wherever you go," she exclaims periodically. " Don't you get very tired? " To which, of course, the obvious answer is that, though we may occasionally lift our eyes to the hills, we are mostly unconscious of their presence, at any rate as impediments. On the journey suburbwards the new houses made themselves everywhere apparent, and Millicent added to her vocabulary the mysterious expression, " ground to *feu*," unknown, apparently, to London!

The sun decided that it might be well to keep on impressing a sceptical Sassenach with a favourable view of a maligned Scottish climate when Millicent made her pilgrimage to view the Forth Bridge, which it has pleased her to designate as the eighth wonder of the world. Cramond, with its picturesque little ferry and the houses clinging to the edge of the cliff, recalled memories of Italian lake-side villages. The crossing safely accomplished, and the interstices of the cottage garden beyond the landing stage negotiated, we found stretched out before us the long walk through the Dalmeny woods.

The trees were as yet only beginning to turn their attention towards a fresh summer toilette, but, otherwise, the walk was perfect. To the right hand the Firth lay blue. The path that wanders with romantic meanderings led us in and out among the trees, now opening out a wide vista of blue water, sparkling in the sunlight, now tantalisingly closing it up again, and leading us in shaded ways. The combined prospect of woods and sea delighted Millicent, reminding her that a journey of some sixty miles was necessary to bring her from her London home to the seaside.

The sun continued to shine, the birds to sing, the water to glisten, but the miles tended rather to lengthen themselves out. To Millicent they must have been somewhat wearisome, following upon her night journey northwards. At length the bridge itself came in sight, and beyond it the welcome tea-room, through whose windows she was able to gaze at the arches.

But Millicent did not devote her entire attention to it. " That girl has a Scottish face," she remarked, indicating a girl in a becoming pink hat at the next table; " but the one with a blue hat hasn't," she added. Pressed to explain the distinction, she pretended that it was impossible to do so. Personally, I feel that a round, rosy countenance comes into the question, but that, remembering

Shakespeare's summing-up—"They are mostly foolish that are so," she has decided that silence is the better part of discretion!

Next day visits to the Castle and Holyrood claimed her attention. The War Memorial made its usual impression. "We have nothing like this," she said, lost in admiration, "we have our Cenotaph, our Unknown Warrior's grave, but nothing like this: no building where everybody's name is written down, where the animals too are remembered—not only the horses and dogs, but the canaries and mice—the tunnellers' friends." She wandered slowly round to reach the culminating point of expression and emotion in the shrine, with its rows of marching men in bronze, each different, individualised. And the fact that the bare rock, the very apex of the Castle rock, should be its pavement, seemed to her entirely and wonderfully fitting. We lingered by the Seasons windows pondering over each little celandine or Christmas rose that has its place beside the scenes of dire import.

Among the historic apartments it was the little bedroom, the birthplace of James, that secured her rapt attention. "I suppose you knew that he was going to be King of England when you gave him this tiny room to be born in!" was her laughingly sarcastic remark.

The Royal Mile, of course, drew her attention next—the washings suspended from the front windows of the houses striking the different note down there. Holyrood she revelled in, with a sigh over the lot of our tragic queen, Mary Stuart.

59

At the Zoo, entertainment there was in plenty, as we passed between the enclosures. For the baboon was pleased to grunt his appreciative grace before food in response to the appeal of a visitor who evidently knew his little idiosyncrasies, and to express his thanks for Millicent's chocolate, which he apparently mistook for a nut, since he retained the cream filling and threw away the " shell." The elephant too, was in frivolous mood, bedecking his back with considerable wisps of straw from his newly-arranged bed. A monkey delighted her by laying hold of a rosy apple, to which he had been paying no previous attention, when the keeper came to clear away the débris of his meal, and springing with it to the roof, holding it in his mouth, secure above all temporary alarms.

Swanston she saw in the perfect peace of Easter Sunday, when the chickens in fawny-coloured broods sheltered beside the mother-hen, and the lambs—two black ones had a special appeal—kept frisking about the mother-sheep. The tiny village, too, was silent, save for the frolics of a child with a puppy, or a cottager stepping out to draw some water from the common tap for a necessary meal. . . .

But it was the hills that kept on impressing her most after London's flatness—the Pentlands, and the Braids, and Blackford, of course, but also the inclines in the streets and roads that you and I never notice. And after these, the spires, that vary and beautify the outline of the buildings against the sky.

II

THE ROUND OF THE YEAR

MISS SNOWDROP COMES TO TOWN

LITTLE Miss Snowdrop has come to town. She wears the simple white dress of a débutante. From her mossy green resting-place in the shop window she looks forth at what the more prosaic among us might call the world of drab realities. I wonder if she feels sadly disillusioned at times, poor little lady!

You see, she must be thinking all the time of that shady nook under the ash tree that was her birthplace, from which she glanced up so timidly—when nobody was there to see—so gratefully, at the giant trees that stood protectingly around her. She looks in vain for the birds that came hopping around in search of an adventurous worm. She listens in vain for the owl that used to hoot with such friendly familiarity when her little white flower-head closed itself up tight and drooped a little lower, under the compelling blanket of night. Yes, Miss Snowdrop has come to town!

She wonders a little at the gay dresses of the daffodils in the adjoining vases—surely they have borrowed something of the sun's own gold. She is impressed by the brilliant robes of purple and scarlet which the tulips have put on to make their curtsey to the new Spring. Perhaps she shrinks from them just the least little bit, for modesty was ever her outstanding characteristic, and, by way of contrast, she fears she may be—shall I call it countrified, just a little unpolished? Quite a delusion, of course, as we should like to tell her in chorus. For in these early days, don't we love her best of all?

Just listen how they greet her, these passers-by who pause, catching sight of her, and at once forget the world of stern realities—mud, slush, east winds. " Oh, look— snowdrops! " they exclaim, and their hearts are lightened at the thought that the winter is nearly ended, that the time of the singing of birds is at hand. "Snowdrops!" they exclaim, and they see—the shop window, the white flowers in little compressed bunches, the gaudy tulips? Oh, no, not at all! For a glimpse at Miss Snowdrop has led them as the song of the thrush led Wordsworth's poor country woman back to other springs. A wood of tall dark trees. The snowdrops in little clumps of white about their roots. Little children, their fingers freezing, joyously gathering them for that sick friend of mother's. . . . A garden where they grew in great profusion all about the lawn, ready to be gathered into these tight bunches for the people of the city, patches of white above the dark earth. . . . Under the gooseberry bushes that fringed a certain garden walk on a night when farewells were in the air. . . . Other white patches of them planted by loving hands, rememberingly, on a grave.

Not all joyful pictures, it is true, but all of them framed in tender thoughts. And so Miss Snowdrop is exchanged for a few pence, eagerly, impetuously, and she is carried away, her dark woods and friendly sparrows behind her, to make a bright moment in somebody's life.

After that I am sure that Miss Snowdrop can never feel lonely or unwanted. The tulips—jealous things!—may be glad of her going since any admiration can now be directed towards themselves. And there is joy over her coming, perhaps to one who is never able to go out to seek her in the woods, or even in the shop-windows. " I have brought you some snowdrops," is the only introduction—if indeed, she requires any at all. Again the pictures rise unbidden out of the slumbering past.

It must either be to a quiet home or to a hospital that Miss Snowdrop is taken. Never, oh, never, would you find her where the clouds of smoke rise in the exotic, artificial atmosphere of the restaurant or the dance hall, or indeed in any place that makes a " feature " of its decorations, floral or otherwise. Lady Tulip, tall and regal, is often there in her purple trappings with appropriate leafy appendages. The Misses Daffodil come there, under the chaperonage of their entanglement of spear-like leaves. Madame Peony, too, who interposes between herself and a possibly chill and ungrateful world, a thick armour of compressed petals. But Miss Snowdrop is never seen there. She would wilt and shrivel up and fade under the changing lights and the heartless music, and the fatuous jesting that camouflages the real and meaningful things of life. She and her first cousin, Miss Violet, would immediately efface themselves in some corner, like the modest little ladies they are.

For Miss Snowdrop was never created to produce a dazzling effect in life. Never was she meant to grace its lordly banquets. Hers is a humbler part. Where the homely teacups come out in a blue and white row and the family circle gathers round at the close of the day, there is Miss Snowdrop in the midst of the table. And old eyes grow young at the sight of her.

Her place, unlike modern woman's, is pre-eminently the home. Perhaps there may come a day when she is solicited to decorate even the formal dinner-table. If she did, I don't think that she would be any longer Miss Snowdrop. Don't you feel that she would suddenly blossom into Lady Whiteflower, or, perhaps, even the Countess of Droopingbells? She prefers, however, that tiny vase on the parlour table where she may catch a glimpse of one of the little birds of St. Francis hopping about the window pane, and where old Mrs. Brown, quietly knitting at the window, looks up for Miss Snowdrop to give her the leading note that, with sudden magic, calls up the days of long ago.

And of course Miss Snowdrop will go, as usual, to the hospitals and nursing homes. Perhaps even now she is being lifted with her sisters from the flower baskets, and is being held in friendly hands in the Royal Infirmary queue—that queue whose emotional output, could it be measured, would reach so high a level. For there is fear in it, though you may not guess it from a superficial glance. Fear of what may be learned when the gate has opened and the great concourse of people has spilled itself into the several doors of the wards. It is a fear that even the message of the snowdrops may do little to lessen. There is joy too, because someone inside has gone within sight of the bourne from which no traveller returns, and

looked across, and—come back. Hopes and desires, re-
grets and good resolutions, all have their place in that
queue that changes daily as regards the units that make it
up but never as regards their emotions.

So Miss Snowdrop comes to the ward. You know,
even before she enters, that her case is hopeless. She will
never come out alive. But *that* is not yet. See how the
tired eyes are turned to greet her. How they smile at her
as she passes by! How the smile deepens into gladness if
she pauses, even for an instant, at a bedside. Just a whiff
of that fresh, earthy smell that tells of resurrected life,
but it is sufficient. Then Miss Snowdrop passes on to
take up a permanent position by some particular bedside
—at least, until the hour comes round when the flowers
are banished to the corridor, for even Miss Snowdrop
may not cheer the loneliness of the ward by night. In the
morning she will return.

She plays the quiet part that has been allotted to her.
Should she " aspire " to the life of a peony, a dahlia, a
rhododendron, can't you imagine the misery and disillusionment that would meet her? But she need not
envy them. There are thousands of pairs of eyes ready to
tell you that, even if the lips that belong to the eyes are
silent.

THE DAFFODIL STORY

In sheets of living gold the story of the daffodils is being told throughout the length and breadth of the country at the present moment. Never before have I seen so many daffodils!

There was a day when I listened to the story which came breaking in upon me, not least impressively amid the mountain silences, as I journeyed from Edinburgh to Oban. Each little suburban garden, each cultivated plot of the wilds, had caught some inkling of the theme— here only a note or two of gold, there a full-toned orchestra of colour. The Brander Pass preferred the simpler explanations of the primroses, wearing their gowns of less conspicuous yellow, as they bunched themselves together among the boulders, peeped so shyly from behind the crannies. But when I penetrated to the wilds of Kilmel fort, and through the woods, still showing their autumn carpets, to lonely Kilchrenan, the story of the daffodils was told again among the tombstones in the garden of sleep.

In the policies of great mansions the gold was heaped together in thick masses; in the shepherd's humble plot it sprinkled itself in single clumps. That was all the difference.

Another day it was the gardens of Peeblesshire that

took up the same golden theme—the trumpet-call of the daffodils, fresh and inspiring, and so uniquely their own. There the manse gardens and the adjoining acres of God repeated it with great understanding. The manse of Newlands, that in autumn days presents a picture so satisfying through the coloured trees, has given its garden a generous sprinkling of the daffodil gold. That of Lyne shows striking massed effects and variations of colour, for the flowers that are crowded so close together in the churchyard and that trail themselves through the manse garden and down the avenue, vary from almost white to deepest daffodil dye. At Stobo the masses of flower gold are protected by rhododendrons, whose scarlet hue is at once arresting and attractive.

But need we go even so far afield for evidence of the widespread circulation of the daffodil story? The tale is repeating itself around our own doorsteps, in the suburban gardens of Edinburgh. How seldom does one set out with the sole object of viewing these gardens unless, perhaps, one happens to be a semi-invalid, with steps necessarily restricted and confined within a narrow radius!

Yet how the daffodils are trumpeting forth, even there, that chorus of *joie de vivre!* One of these gardens has attempted, even within its narrow boundaries, a massed effect, and presents the familiar sheet of gold interspersed with wallflowers, so that, when the daffodils fade, the garden shall not be left desolate. There are few gardens that do not possess their clumps of daffodils.

Other colours are in evidence, white and purple being popular at the moment. Peeping through a garden gate,

I see them combined in a bed of arabis and aubrietia beside the front door. In the next garden I find a row of stiffly-upholstered hyacinths, pink and blue and yellow, thick-set amid a border of daffodils and wallflowers. Rhododendron blossoms, pale pink or deep rose, are brightening with their glow many a dark corner. A purple fringe of aubrietia has hung itself about the bow window of one of the newer houses—and indeed it is amazing how soon these bungalows have unrolled their floral carpets free from bare patches! But while one's eyes are grateful for all their colour and their light, it is to the daffodils that they return for that feeling of special " uplift ".

Isn't it just because they are so human? Wordsworth, long ago, recognized that message of sheer joy. And, at the moment, all broad Scotland knows it too.

IN AN OLD-WORLD GARDEN

June is, or at least it ought to be, emphatically the month of gardens. The public gardens call us to partake of their sweetness and their rich displays of colour. Their plots, nowadays, hold less regard for conventionalism, and have decided to include flowers other than the scarlet geraniums, yellow calceolarias, and the blue lobelia of yore.

We suburbanites render thanks daily—if we do not forget to do so—for our little square yards of gardens, with their ordered array of flowers, glad of their colour and their freshness, but rejoicing, perhaps, less than did the gardeners of other years in their perfume, which used to include the illimitable mystery of musk and southernwood, the satisfaction of lavender. The roses of the past were veritable bowls of perfume. Now, with newer and greater variety in their colourings, they have lost much of it—and many of their petals.

The town garden keeps as the chief end in front of it— orderliness. Regularly in due season the " potted " plants come out of their pots or their wrappings to replace those whose season is over. If even a pansy transgresses this law of order by merely overstepping its territory by the matter of an inch or two, it suffers for its error, as likely as not, by being uprooted and thrown out altogether. For the suburbanite must have order. How else should he manage the small space allotted to him? There is little room for lilacs and laburnums, less for mysterious nooks and crannies, even in the larger gardens, if the tulips and the asters and the chrysanthemums are, each in due season, to receive the honour they deserve.

Even the perfume of the flowers brings less of unbounded longing that it held in other less conventional gardens. The emotions aroused are cribbed, cabined, and confined by the exigencies of space. There is little room in the suburban garden for the fragrant wistfulness aroused by the whiff of southernwood, that makes the scent of " Nuit de Noel " or " Vers le Jour " recall just the factory at Grasse, or perhaps merely the shop of the perfumier.

There are times, however, when the perfume is potent enough to waft us back to the days when it did have illimitable meaningfulness. Perhaps it was an old-world garden, wet with the dew of morning and glittering in the sunlight—and the sun knew how to shine in those days!—that one passed through, setting out for school. How attractive and alluring it looked on these mornings of June, with the near prospect of compressed desks and dismal mathematical formulæ to blot it out! Never did a garden look more desirable as a place to linger in than on a morning such as that.

I recall, too, a garden, on the homeward way, belonging to a little cottage hidden in a wood, a cottage over which the real old-fashioned cabbage roses clambered and hung, great cupfuls of sweetness. The old lady who lived there—her hair had a glitter of the sun about it—used to welcome the children who stopped in passing to admire her roses, filling their hands with flowers. (She also allowed them to sample her raspberry jam. Nor have I ever seen raspberries that grew like hers did.) If I return to that cottage now, I am assured that I shall find but a heap of stones, a garden overgrown with weeds, perhaps a few raspberry canes growing wild, never a trace of the great pink roses. Yet memory and perfume persist in spite of, sometimes even more powerfully because of, disillusionment.

There was another garden of long ago that I might call the children's garden. How difficult it is to give up a garden! Continually I am hearing people tell me how much harder it is than to give up even a house of memories. This old garden was a place much loved by the children and their pets in summer time. It was an old-world garden where the children played, trundling their toy carts about the walks, giving an unwilling pussy-cat a ride in one of them, or selecting as passenger and victim a more accommodating dolly. The garden walks were bordered with boxwood that grew to the dimensions of a miniature hedge. The pet rabbits also contributed to their entertainment—and to the sorrows of their childhood, when death came to them unexpectedly.

There came times when the children decided that something really must be done to improve the condition of the garden. It was just as different from the orderly bedded-out parterres of the suburban villa as one so-called garden could be from another. The latter sees its plots decked in properly-disposed white or gold when the snowdrops or the crocuses spangle the earth in spring; the geraniums redden there in summer, and the lobelia stars the beds with blue; in autumn the tall chrysanthemums and dahlias clothe the garden right regally. In that garden none of these things happened at all properly.

No plant therein cherished any kind of respect for the territory of any other. A yellow briar rose sprouted up just anywhere and everywhere. Honesty made little purple patches all over the place. You met the columbine at the door, held tight in the embrace of a male fern; at a little distance you found it to be on equally intimate terms with the pansies and the irises. By the time autumn came, when the peonies had faded and the roses were tearing themselves away in a lingering farewell, a few spikes of montbretia alone proclaimed themselves out of a hopeless muddle of greenery.

It was usually in the spring-time that the children's good intentions asserted themselves. The plants had but lately shown themselves out of the brown earth, and the task was a simpler one. I remember one whole day which the children devoted to the rockery, lifting the stones and rearranging them, seeking to restrain the encroaching tendencies of a blue periwinkle, to leave a little room for the white violets that were so sweet and so compressed. Then they started on the walks, pruning the tiresome box-wood and dragging up the weeds. Next day school called them again, and ere another tidying-up fit seized them, the task had grown far beyond what their puny efforts could hope to cope with.

Just now, I think, the peonies are flaunting themselves

in these old-fashioned gardens—they are far too big for the modern garden plot. Their lure is not made because of their perfume, but by many they are well loved. Sweet-williams, too, with the stiffness of their upholstered effects, their tight prim little heads, their curious velvety mixtures of colour, are joining them. Columbine—it also delights in variegated effects—is running wild everywhere. The roses about to open out are the yellow briar roses, the old-fashioned blush pink roses, the big cabbage ones. . . . Only one's eyes must feast instead on the city gardens, and appear greatly content therewith until, one day, a sniff of perfume . . . and memory gets to work again.

I suppose there are still gardens even such as that! Only one needs to know them to realize that they may give more happiness than even the gardens that are best ordered.

The gardens of final rest—they have their flowers too. Nor are their flowers wholly conventional, though there was Mrs. Johnson of " Handasyde's " book about gardens, who preferred a weeping willow to a grave covered with daffodils. " The homely wallflower that is to rise again," the writer tells us, " appeals more to simple folk than the white celestial lily; for country people are sometimes afraid of the long journey they must take all alone, and like to think they will be greeted at the end by the face of some old familiar friend."

FALLING LEAVES

DURING these last few days the city trees have been, in some cases extensively, robbed of their clothing. Last week they still clung to the green of summer—a somewhat dingy and tired-looking green, I admit. Then, suddenly, in a night, the fairy of the transforming wand had changed their dress to gold. Others she had dealt with more harshly, leaving them mere bare skeletons of their former selves.

"It is impossible," the fairy of the transforming and devastating wand seemed to say, "you need not deceive yourselves any longer. Winter is coming, fast and sure." So it was not inappropriate that, just at the same time, we carried out that little operation with our clocks that gave us the early dark evenings. The facility with which that change is now accomplished is surely but another example of the mechanism of habit.

Time was, perhaps, when we rather marvelled at each other when, an hour of sleep omitted, we kept our engagements on the first morning of Summer Time. Time was, perhaps, when, having accepted back that extra hour, we stole downstairs with a somewhat guilty feeling on the first morning of Winter Time. Of the change nowadays it might be said that "it puts us neither up nor down." Not infrequently we forget even to comment upon it!

Now, through the falling leaves, we daily pursue our occupations. Beneath them the students pass to their classes—and with their return this week the city resumes its full winter stride. For them, I fancy, the falling leaves are a happy omen. Life is in front of them; anything might happen; the gates of Faery are still wide open. The coming winter may summon up a picture of examinations and midnight oil consumption; it has also another side which shows much social intercourse, the meeting of kindred spirits, the unlocking of thoughts that have, hitherto, been too precious to pass the doors of one's own heart. For from the discussion of generalities, of philosophies of the why and the wherefore of the universe, one inevitably passes to questioning the why and wherefore of the individual, of the self. To share these thoughts with understanding friends is the privilege of student days. A time so opportune probably never occurs again.

But not alone do the students go forth gaily under the yellowing trees. There is young Mrs. Smith, whose mind is buoyed up not inconsiderably by the prospect of the new hat, the quest of which is her reason for thus gaily tripping forth. To the office-girls who tread with their immaculate footwear upon the fallen leaves, there comes a vision of the filmy frocks and silver shoes that are to be theirs for the whirl of the dance. The afternoon sunshine entices old Mrs. Brown to take a walk, leaning on the arm of her daughter, under the falling leaves. She must make the most of the sunshine, for there will come sunless winter afternoons when she can only view the world from her parlour window.

But, unfortunately, there is another aspect of the falling leaves. There comes a day when the sun refuses to set their gold a-glittering, when the chill raw coldness of a dull depressing atmosphere makes devastating inroads upon our mental outlook. In our vision, then, we see neither silver slippers nor the blest communion of soul with soul. Instead, an endless succession of dreary days —life. Each one of them filled with its own ritual of dressing, eating, working, and then sinking again into sleep. A new hat—yes, but it will not keep its freshness or its novelty. The silver slippers will tarnish and lose their elasticity. Even the sun will presently hide itself from our eyes. To each day its duties. True—but so much that we do to-day has to be done over again to-morrow.

The housewife's work, for example—and it is well if she can keep her thoughts off this particular train. The dish-washing of to-day has to be repeated to-morrow, and on through seemingly endless to-morrows. So, with the food-making, the cleaning-up, the turning-out of rooms. Even those whose work is a process of development, the artist's for instance, sometimes lose heart; how much more dreary hers that is a continual repetition of what she has done before? The teacher's too, starting each year over again with a new class, repeating the work of the previous year. So with most of us—continual repetition, the necessity of rousing ourselves to fresh interest in things that might long ago seem to have lost their savour.

The falling leaves, on a dreary day, have an unpleasant

way of suggesting the futility of things. " Look at us,"
they say, " see how fresh and green we were in spring-
time—how alluring, how radiant! Look at us now,
fading, dying, soon to be trodden under foot in the slush
of the street, passing-away, forgotten." Oh, naughty,
insinuating autumn leaves!

Only the very young, I think, are inclined to take that
message over-seriously. Only the very young are too
much inclined to listen to the Byronic plaint of the " sere
and yellow leaf." Others with more experience of life
will not find the seeming message of the leaves too dis-
illusioning. The mood, they know, will pass. Life's
monotony, they find, is constantly being lit, by little experiences, little happenings, that make its joy. Flowers
of interest keep springing up all along the way, else,
surely, we might all sit down by the wayside and weep
over its fatuity. The message of the falling leaves on a
dreary day, though it does give us to think, is not to be
dwelt upon too seriously.

But does not the knowledge that there is this side to
autumn, and that it may thrust itself uppermost at any
moment, make brighter its other aspects? The glory of
its elating colour-schemes owes not a little of its wonder
to its under-current of sadness.

THE MESSAGE OF THE POPPY

Down in Lady Haig's Poppy Factory in the Canongate,
the scarlet flowers of remembrance have been growing
within recent days under the fingers of disabled soldiers.
They have taken the little petals of silk and lawn and
paper, the green leaves, the button with its differentiating
stamp for the centre, the cocoanut fibre for the stamens,
and they have united them, over and over again, to make
a poppy. But they are greater than mere makers of
artificial flowers, these quiet-looking men, for into each
poppy they have woven the magic that ensnares the recipient in a mesh of dreams.

Forth into a world held in November's dreary grasp
go the poppies that they have created. And at sight of
them the thoughts rush backward to the days that were;
the mind goes a-dreaming down the years.

*　　　*　　　*　　　*

Boom! The two minutes' silence had begun.

She sat in church, the flowers of remembrance in front
of her. In spirit she was far away. Again, she, his
mother, was standing in the war-cemetery near Ypres,
where the air was clover-scented and the stones rose in
long white rows, their guardian rose-trees beside them,
the blue lobelia crouched beneath. Through the silence

80

the questions came surging, as is their way in graveyards, to receive no answer. Only the sounds of the reapers came to her, busy with their hooks in the field beyond the hedge.

She was kneeling now to take a picture of the little stone that, only to her, was different from all the surrounding stones. The bees were busy in the clover, among the rose-leaves. To them this garden of sleep was just like other gardens: it offered the possibility of hidden sweetness.

But that was in summer-time. The roses would have faded now. The wreath of poppies that she had sent out would be lying on the dank, sodden ground. No bees would care for these flowers.

*   *   *   *

From Flanders fields, where memory's poppies grow so abundantly each November, her dream carried her back to the night when he went away—a dull November night, that too. They were sitting at home, engaged in their ordinary occupations, not knowing that the call would come so soon. His father was reading the newspaper with its interminable casualty lists. His young sister was busy with her home-lessons. She, herself, was sewing as usual.

Then he came in.

He did not say anything at first. He made the customary casual remarks about the weather, with which we seek to hide our deeper emotions. She noticed that his cheeks were pale. There was a tense unfamiliar look about his eyes. And suddenly she was afraid.

Then he told them. . . . To-morrow!

Before her there flashed the succession of endless to-morrows, in which he would not come. His young sister, thrilled with excitement, looked up from her French exercise and exclaimed, " So you're really going at last! " The dull length of the days in barracks was at an end.

He had not said much. He had not even stayed to supper. She had tried to curb her feelings—would there not be all these unending to-morrows after he had gone, in which she could let them have their way? But her lips had faltered. He had noticed it and tried to brace her up with cheery remarks, forced mirth. He had gone forth bravely into the unknown—though she noticed how he fumbled for the door-handle.

" It won't be long till I get leave," was what he said.

Then the door had closed.

When he was gone, his young sister, realising that something beyond her powers of comprehension had taken place, broke out into miserable sobbing.

And she had taken up the sewing that had slipped from her grasp, and worked her needle furiously in and out, in a vain attempt to stifle that dull ache at her heart.

* * * *

Again the years moved backward. It was the morning when he first went to school. He had buckled on his bag so joyfully, after seeing that his one precious book was safe and secure within. He had buttoned up his new coat with undisguised pride, fitting each button carefully into the appropriate hole—that had never happened a second time! She had watched him go from the door

with a little ache at her heart even then—the first of re-
nunciation's links was being severed. But he had gone
forth unfalteringly into the unknown, murmuring with
a little backward look, as if he understood, " It won't be
long till night, mummie."

She watched him growing through the years until, in
the full strength of manhood, he stood before her once
again, buttoning on his soldier's uniform.

*　　　*　　　*　　　*

Boom! The two minutes' silence was over.

She gazed round the church. It was the people in the
pews who were the shadows, the unreal. Like the ghosts
of a dream she saw them rise to join in the hymn " For
all the saints who from their labours rest."

The dead were not dead but alive. The poppy had
wrought the miracle. " It won't be long," he seemed to
be whispering still.

CHRISTMAS DECISIONS

THE other evening I happened to look in at Florence's to find that, in some ways, my visit was not ill-timed. She was in the throes of mating her Christmas gifts to their respective future owners; surrounded by all manner of objects, ranging from a Teddy bear to the most minute of pin-bowls, there she stood. Her presents covered the dining-room table; they littered the chairs; they spilled themselves over on the floor. And there was Florence, her pretty face slightly perturbed, the waves of her hair just a little ruffled, surveying the disorder around her.

" Oh, don't apologise! " she exclaimed, when I suggested that perhaps I had arrived inopportunely, " I'm sure you can help me. You've no idea how difficult it is. Or—have you? I suppose everybody must go through it. I'm so horribly afraid of sending the wrong things— no, of sending the right things to the wrong people—you know what I mean. I've been thinking so hard that my head is beginning to throb," and she stroked it tenderly. " Now, do sit down, and I'll tell you all about it." Which she proceeded to do—at considerable length.

" We went for a lovely motor run this afternoon— Fred and I," was her apparently irrelevant introduction. " It was really wonderful driving back from Peebles.

Do you know how the big Christmas moon shines down on the dark fir trees? He seems to be whispering all the most romantic kind of thoughts to them—such companionable thoughts, the secrets that they were going to share about Christmas, secrets of which we humans may get a mere inkling, no more." ("She's really off!" I murmured to myself, having had previous experience of these rhapsodisings of Florence's!) "But even that was enough to make me understand just a little—something about the spirit of Christmas, that romantic feeling that never comes to you at any other season of the year. It's the same kind of feeling that we used to have about Santa Claus and hanging up our stockings. I felt that I should love to go on for ever—with Fred—just looking at the moon and these fir trees standing out so clearly against the twilight sky."

Yes, she seemed about to become immersed in one of her day-dreams. I saw it dawning in her misty eyes, and my time was precious. "But—all these?" I interrupted gently, indicating the heterogeneous collection of articles that lay around us.

"Oh, yes, I'm coming to them. Well, I thought when I came home that I was just in the most blissful condition for sending off my presents, radiating peace and goodwill, love towards humanity—even to Aunt Jane—you know the kind of feeling? So I banished Fred to a friend's, and I got out all the things I had collected, but somehow I just can't fit them to people. It's like a jig-saw puzzle, and here am I amidst confusion worse confounded!"

" What a lovely jug! " I exclaimed involuntarily—it was I who was irrelevant now. Pale yellow, painted with crocuses of mauve and purple and saffron, it had caught the sunny spirit of springtime, and held on to it even in mid-winter.

" Yes, isn't it? " replied Flo. " I got that for Aunt Jane. But does she like crocuses, or doesn't she? You know these intense likes and dislikes of hers. When she comes here I spend every minute trying to steer clear of them—the dislikes, I mean. There were others equally fascinating—yellow jugs bordered with pink wild roses —or was it apple blossom? Clusters of cherries on a blue ground, tulips growing up like these crocuses—adorable things! Marmalade jars, all sprayed about with tiny garlands of flowers. Morning sets, bright yellow. I've got the yellow fever to-day—it's such a refreshing, cheering-up, ' all's right with the world ' kind of colour. But Aunt Jane had jaundice once upon a time. . . ."

" Oh, for goodness sake, don't! " I interrupted, " who is to be the recipient of this very useful object? " It was a cookery book that I had picked up.

" Well, I had Cousin Margaret in mind when I bought that," she replied, " but she's so ' touchy ' and she prides herself on the excellence of her cakes, the superiority of her pies. Cooking is the be-all and the end-all of existence to her—she lives in the kitchen. I could think of nothing more appropriate to send her. But since I got it I've begun to doubt my wisdom. You see she may be offended, taking it as a suggestion that her recipes may really be improved upon."

"My child," I interrupted, "you are becoming absolutely morbid! Certainly Margaret must have her cookery book, so that's that! And this pretty thing?" I indicated a teapot stand of mosaic-like pattern, in which blue and green predominated.

"Oh, that," she said, her face brightening, "have you seen the new shop where they sell Oriental things—these bricks, Arab glass—a deep blue it is—Maltese lace, Eastern robes—delightful for fancy dress—Oriental scents in funny tubes; all kinds of things? Really I like that so well that I think I must keep it for myself. And I had intended it for Betty. I must just get another for her."

"Of course, you must!" I agreed, cheerfully—there are moments when one feels that Florence is made for no other end than to be petted and stroked the right way. "After all"—there should have been a twinkle in my eye—"couldn't most of us make a better job of choosing our own presents than other people succeed in accomplishing?"

"They certainly couldn't do worse than I'm doing," Florence relapsed into the querulous vein, "and with the best intentions in the world! Look at these coloured hankies—aren't they lovely?" and she held out the flimsy squares of georgette. "I love to look at all these colours together. But, of course, I can't afford to give each of my friends a whole boxful—more's the pity—and now, it's the colour trouble again. Everybody, I suppose, would like a pink one or a blue one—there are Pam and Joan who have sworn never to wear any other colour. But the green, the yellow, the flame—suppose they don't match?"

There are moments too when, talking to Florence, one feels at least a hundred years old!

"My *dear* child," was my inevitable response, "anybody would love to have any one of these soft lovely colours," and I held up a dainty wisp of apple-green silk.

"Oh, well, it is nice of you to say so. I won't worry any more about them. But," her brows were beginning to pucker again, "books are difficult too. I seem to think that all my friends should like the same kind of books that I do myself—and they don't. I've sent just the loveliest things before now, and afterwards I've heard, indirectly, that they just didn't fit in. Of course, it's only my second-best friends. I hope the others are all right. Now, everybody must like 'Omar'?"

"I'm not quite sure," I murmured, not over-anxious to throw out further doubts for this feminine Thomas to lay hold upon.

"Anyhow, Aunt Mary's going to get him," exclaimed Florence, assuming a mood of reckless bravado. "And this needle-case is for Gladys. She isn't keen on sewing, but now that she's a mother, a little encouragement won't do her any harm. The teddy is for the baby. And the pink butterfly brooch is for Alice Morison. Only I'm rather afraid it's helio she prefers. And, oh, Cynthia, this is my very latest discovery!"

She opened a cardboard box and displayed a fascinating set of table mats in the form of sycamore leaves, in natural green with one giant leaf for the serving-mat—a stroke of genius on the part of the man or woman who first thought of the idea. It must give one a delightfully picnicky kind of feeling to lunch off a leaf!

"I'd love to keep these, but"—assuming an air of firmness—"I shall send them to Mary Ferguson. She was married just a few months ago, and she'll love to have all the newest things, whereas old married people like myself——" And she pretended to heave a sigh. The time will never come when Florence will appear a day older than Mary Ferguson, and she knows it quite well!

"Men's presents are the most difficult of all," sighed Florence. "And they don't give one any pleasure in choosing them—no colourful sensations, no whiffs of perfume, no thrills. But I've got socks for Fred, and the new steel-shaft club, and a tie for George, and cigarettes for Tom, and——"

"Well, now you've got them all nicely fixed up, I'll depart," I said, beginning to put on my gloves. "I've got my own presents to wrap up."

"You've helped me quite a lot," replied Florence. "But—oh, these hankies! Was it green or yellow that Maisie liked?"

I could see that she was on the point of starting it all over again, so I departed, wondering if my own decisions would be as difficult to arrive at!

"RING OUT THE OLD . . ."

TWELVE o'clock was drawing near. The Old Year was very weary. But he managed to pull himself together. He must make an effort, for soon it would be too late— saddest of words. He sat up and rubbed his eyes. He began to soliloquise.

"Oh, dear, I am tired," I imagined I heard him say, while I was waiting for the bells that were to herald the birth of the New Year, "How flat and depressing things get just before the end! Time to fade away, sure enough —I couldn't stand much more of this kind of existence! I heard a mortal announce the other day, as if he thought he was saying something really original and weighty, that it was the aftermath of Christmas that was afflicting the world. Well, if they've eaten too much plum pudding they needn't blame *me* for that! Its memories, these handed in by the postman, will last long after its indigestion has passed into the limbo of forgotten things. Christmas supplies a useful enough purpose in that it makes us take an annual census of our friends."

"There was another mortal," he went on, "who breathed a little prayer of thankfulness to the Christmas spirit the other evening. A friend of hers had been sick, sick unto death, for weeks, and a grief-distraught household, while the balance sways this way and that, have little inclination to write letters, to communicate to paper the fears that are seething in their minds. But when Christmas comes the letter-writing can be put off no longer. So are the dropped stitches caught up again, and the weaving of the pattern proceeded with."

"Oh, dear! Oh, dear!" He continued to rub his eyes, "how they leave me alone, these mortals, to die forgotten, neglected!" I think he saw, as by a flashlight then, the crowd at the Tron! "And I haven't really been such a bad year to them after all! True, I nearly froze everybody up in February—how I enjoyed playing that prank upon them!—I was young then! But I made up for it afterwards—really I always try to do that. Think of the March sunshine I gave them! And the gorgeous days of July! And the wonder of the golden September evenings. And the October afternoons with their red sunsets! Of course," here he hung his head a little, "November wasn't very good but," brightening up, "it must rain sometimes. Really, I haven't been too bad to them, and yet, here I am, left alone to die—all their thoughts are given to that little blue-eyed stranger the New Year. I wonder if they honestly believe that *he* can do much better?"

The mists were creeping about his eyes now, as he settled himself to his final rest. But just before the end I think the hubbub of the riotous crowds became muffled: the picture of midnight streets and black bottles faded, and before his dying eyes a series of quieter visions presented themselves. . . .

The Old Year opened his dying eyes the smallest fraction of an inch—it cost him an effort even to achieve so much now, but the compulsion was irresistible. And he saw a young man, strong and handsome, with the light of a great purpose shining in his eyes.

" Good Old Year," he was whispering to himself. " You haven't been so bad, have you, old fellow? There was that exam."—and the light in his eyes burned fiercer, and showed the strength and determination there. " If I hadn't passed that, well, I'd jolly well have been done for! It meant simply the making or marring of my career. Of course, I made up my mind to get through " —and the Old Year noted the resolution that would carry him through any obstacles that the New Year and the other years might place before him. " But still you let me do it, Old Year, and no other year can have the honour. Here! " He seized his glass. " I'll jolly well drink to the year that is (nearly) awa', and the others can attend to the health of the new-born infant."

And the slowly-fading light of the Old Year flickered a little brighter, because, old though we may be, we are never insusceptible to praise! . . .

Then there came a woman. She was young in years, but the light of youth had faded from her eyes that held a great sorrow. She wore a black robe and she carried lilies, symbolic of the stainless little life that had passed from her.

" Good-bye, Old Year," she whispered, calm and quiet now in her sadness. " You will always be the most precious of years to me, because you shared my baby with me. Oh, I don't want to find that she belongs to the things that are past." Her eyelids drooped. "Oh, Old Year, can't you, can't you stay?"

Curiously stirred by her petition, he made an effort to raise himself, inspired by a desire to give consolation and courage. But the vision with drooped head had faded away. Another had taken her place. . . .

A girl, radiant with happiness. She wore some blue drapery, the heaven's colour, symbolic of hope, and her golden hair clustered about her head in curls. She turned to him a smiling face, and, as he looked at her, he felt that life had, perhaps, not been in vain.

"Old Year, I want to whisper my secret," she said, and her beauty became more dream-like as she looked at him. "You are the best, the sweetest year, that ever was born! Always I shall love you, and every Old Year's Night it is *you* that I shall remember! I want to thank you, Old Year. I want to go on thanking you for ever and ever and ever!" She would have said more—a great deal more!—but instinct seemed to tell her that the sands were running low. "You see, Old Year, Frank has just told me—that—he—loves me!"

And because of her charm and her sweetness, the Old Year made the final supreme effort. He opened his eyes and flashed her a look of joyous sympathy. Then he fell back exhausted. . . .

And just then the bells crashed out. The New Year had arrived. The infant year had been born, and his is the duty of dealing with us mortals now, to make or mar our happiness. Somehow, we can't take to him very kindly just at once.   He is a stranger, knowing nothing of our joys or our sorrows.

But, doubtless, we shall soon become better acquainted!

III

IN PENSIVE VEIN

GHOSTS OF THE PAST

WHAT would life be without its ghosts, these shadowy phantom forms in which our memories take shape? The ghosts of the past! They are for the most part, nice friendly ghosts, like that grey-clad shade of Mary Rose. They have nothing about them of the malevolence of a fearsome " boggit " which I heard Mr. Mortimer Batten describe some time ago, as haunting an old Border manor house. Sometimes they may be rather sad, just a little bit wistful-eyed, bringing with them something of the longing of the saddest thoughts with which our sweetest songs are haunted. Sometimes they are entirely gay.

These ghosts of the past belong solely to ourselves. Such is the prerogative of ghosts. We alone can see them. Others may share our memories with us. They may breathe the same scent of violets, inhale the same fragrance of lavender. But our reactions will differ from theirs just as subtly in the one case as in the other. We see our own ghosts.

And, without them, what a dull world this would be! Maeterlinck has made of his Land of Memory a very sweet and restful place, and so should it always be. We forget so often that we are living in it all the time. We

G

admire a particular picture, forgetting that most of its charm lies, not in itself, but in that power in us, worked up out of experiences that have gone before, that enables us to appreciate it. So with a piece of music; it speaks to us only when memories are linked up with it. Ourselves, we are walking bundles of memories that affect and colour each new experience; that play upon it and adapt it until it is assimilated with the rest.

And of these memories, grey shadowy ghosts of people and happenings, a richer crop than that produced by almost any other after-sowing is yielded up by our schooldays. They may be bitter or sweet, for it is a mistake to imagine that childhood—Ellen Montgomery, for one, will bear me out in this!—is always a happy period : suffering can be very acute, entirely devastating, when the lamp of experience has not yet been lighted to show that the sorrow will fade out and life become normal once again.

Sometimes when coming in contact with other gatherings of ex-school-girls, ranging from grandmotherly matrons down to youthful " flappers ", I have felt tempted to envy them the happy atmosphere in which they met. Yet the ghosts that assemble at an annual festivity can scarcely meet in such formidable array as those that gather together after having been in restraint for years, and are suddenly let loose to work their will. So did I find the other day, on returning to my old school, which used to appear many miles from Edinburgh, and which, in these days of changing distances, now seems quite near, to take leave of the rector who has presided over its progress from infancy to maturity.

And the ghosts that come to us then?—

" When we look back and forgetfully wonder
What we were like in our work and our play."

Just quite humble little ghosts. Wisps of impressions, shadowy figments of events, memories that faded out almost before they had been born, intangible, fleeting. Ghosts of early days—one brought me a glimpse of a small child reading a list of library books in a glass case before penetrating into the room of the head-master to tell him that she wanted to learn French and Latin—a very undistinguished ghost indeed!

Ghosts of lessons, some that were anticipated with nervous apprehension and that wove a black pattern into the sampler of school-life; others that were merely grey, the lessons to which one was indifferent; others still that were outstanding and that were woven in in brightly coloured threads.

Your ghosts may be different from mine. They may lean to realism rather than to romance. But I should choose these that bring me back memories of Horatius and his brave deeds and the eagle's nest on purple Apennine, or of Linden on which " all bloodless lay the untrodden snow," or even of Lord Ullin's daughter. We can smile at them now, these rather wistful ghosts, that hankered after romance, but, in these days, they were very real! Ghosts of the French lesson—there is one of them that visits me now and again. Why it insists on lingering about I know not, but it keeps on repeating, over and over again, a haunting line about eyes:—

> "Ils dorment au fond du tombeau,
> Et le soleil se lève encore."

I think it must be seeking always to lead my thoughts back to the war years, and to a certain Roll of Honour upon the school-wall. For those who were at school before the war are haunted by ghosts more poignant than most. In school-days the grey flutter of the wings of death seems so distant that we are almost tempted to believe that it may pass us by. It is the way of youth thus to think, and yet the youth of that generation was to become upon very familiar terms with death, and that, in many cases, while scarcely escaped from the school-room. Death came to them, bringing honour and the solution of the mysteries that we who are left are still waiting to solve. It is inevitable that we should quote:—

> "They shall not grow old as we that are left grow old,
> Age shall not weary them, nor the years condemn."

And again, remembering them, isn't there Maurice Baring to remind us, that when our own paths grow difficult, they

> "Will speed us onward with a cheer,
> And wave beyond the stars that all is well."

Grey ghosts of examinations—they keep surging up, bringing perhaps the little thrill of a success, the dull ache that followed a failure. Ghosts of exhibition days, their palms and lilies, their white schoolgirl frocks and frizzed out hair, and the subtle, unsatisfying sense of non-fulfilment—perhaps such characterises most " endings ". Along with them there comes the pale ghost of an earlier exhibition day, before one was initiated, when one was dazzled by the brilliancy of those able to speak French, and humbled by references to Latin and Greek and Euclid (was it another language?) so that that " inferiority complex ", if it had been invented in those days, would have become devastatingly busy. A shadowy memory, too, looms up of the drill-sergeant who was wont to wound one's susceptibilities, for little girls did not always move with military precision. Strange how human, how kindly, even drill-sergeants can appear in the after years!

Towering above the shadowy ghosts of feelings and sensations often rise those of teachers and of school-friends. Teachers had their part in making us what we are—a part that can never be over-emphasised. Theirs was the task of working upon that plastic, mouldable putty of our minds. And somehow these teachers of the past seem more real than the same teachers standing before us in flesh and blood.

With our teachers that were, we scarcely feel at home. There is a nasty little ghost of jealousy entering somewhere! In the days that are past, it was we who mattered. Endless successions of boys and girls have done their best to blot us out from their memories. Our memories of school are those of—how many years ago? Our teachers are, inevitably, more up-to-date.

The ghosts of school-friends. Out of the shades they come because in this environment we used to meet and mingle with them. The room becomes peopled with the girls and boys of the past. For there are no friends like those of our school-days. One makes friends more easily than ever in after life, and such friendships have an infinitely stronger chance to endure. We may meet them but seldom, yet there is always the common bond that is enduring, and at any chance encounter the tongues will at once become unloosed, the old inconsequent chatter set itself flowing.

The ghosts, I hope, were satisfied at the reception of their heaped-up memories. They will continue to come again as single spies, but seldom, as on that recent occasion, in battalions.

THE ROSE-COLOURED COSY

ROSALIE first saw it in an Edinburgh shop window, where large red tickets directed the attention of passers-by to sales' bargains—Rosalie isn't really her name, but it matches the cosy. Rose-coloured, dazzlingly cheerful, it stood between a tea-cosy that was self-sufficiently blue and another that was over-consciously purple. The pink cosy, less selfishly inclined, shed its brightening glow all around.

Rosalie looked at it and pondered. She wanted a tea-cosy of her own, or, at least, she would want one when she acquired the new set of teacups. And, of course, of all colours under the sun, her cosy should be of the altruistic rose-colour. The cosy wasn't expensive—unless regarded from the point of view that anything that is not immediately required for use *is* expensive. But if she took it home, what would Auntie say? She might consider it an open-eyed insult to her brown and green veteran of many years' service. Rosalie felt sure she would. She would also complain that Rosalie was wasting her money, seeing that he had spent it on a tea-cosy rather than on a box of chocolates! Aunties are strange people.

Rosalie passed on. She did one or two errands of a depressingly mundane nature. It was a dull, dreary day

—greyness everywhere. The streets were slushy, rain kept threatening to fall; it was a thoroughly January-ish day—worse to endure than a November-ish one. To cheer herself Rosalie went to a florist's window at the West End, just to see how much farther on his bulbs were than her own.

She came back to the window that held the rose-coloured cosy. She recalled past experiences. "Yes," she ruminated, "if I don't buy it to-day, I'll probably spend hours hunting all over the town when I do actually require it, and, in the end, have to be content with a second best." She recalled, too, that she who hesitates is lost. She determined to be one of the ninety-and-nine. She went in and bought the cosy.

That might have been the end of the tale. In ordinary circumstances, the cosy would have been a cosy, rose-coloured indeed, but nothing more. Auntie would have received it, not with open arms, not invitingly, perhaps even frostily, but she might have thawed immediately under the sunshine of Rosalie's smile. Unfortunately, Rosalie forgot to smile.

It is ever a problem whether these women who stay indoors or those who go out to work have more reason—if anyone ever has reason—to become victims of nerves. In most circumstances the vote would go to the former. But, by tea-time, under the genial influence of a comfortable fire, an easy chair, and a spread tea-table, they might be supposed to have laid them for a little. Unfortunately, just before tea-time, the nerves of the worker-who-goes-out-and-has-just-come-in are at their rawest. All kinds of little worries had beset Rosalie that day, and, finally, a snowball had hit her as she alighted from the tram.

At the tea-table, she displayed the tea-cosy. She chose her moment indiscreetly, that I admit. Perhaps she, too, knew that the time was not propitious, but a certain little demonaic devotee of the creed that things-are-so-bad-that-they-can't-be-any-worse prompted her. Anyhow, she undid the wrappings and waited for the disapproval that was sure to come.

"Oh," said Auntie, "what did you buy that for? We don't need it." "But it isn't for you," objected Rosalie, "it is mine." "But it will soil so easily," said Auntie, "why couldn't you have chosen a darker colour?" It was Miss Brown, however, Auntie's bosom friend, who gave the most unkindest cut of all. From her Rosalie expected such mildly approving epithets as "dainty", "very pretty", "quite nice". What Miss Brown actually said was, "You must put a white cover over it. It *won't wash*."

"Put a white cover over my rose-coloured cosy!" exclaimed Rosalie, thoroughly roused. "Why to look at it is as good as a tonic! You put white covers over all your bright colours, and buy bottles of medicine as a result!" But as Auntie still continued to air her grievance about the cosy not being required, and Miss Brown continued to advocate the advantages of white, washable covers, Rosalie—I grieve to relate the fact!—subsided into tears.

A storm in a teacup, I quite admit. All over a silly tea-cosy—yes, I quite agree. But how many of our ordinary every-day upheavals have any weightier an origin?

There is much to be said for Auntie—I hear the older ladies in chorus. And quite a lot to be said for Rosalie, only she might have managed things better, is the more modern chorus. (Did tears go out of fashion with the arrival of the powder-puff and the lipstick?) Auntie adheres to the fashions in vogue in her " day ". She detests table-runners and dinner mats, and even teacloths laid on cross-wise, and couches that stick out, and pianos that maintain any other than a rigid position straight against the wall.

And Rosalie, while she lives in Auntie's house—though contributing generously to its upkeep, knows that she must, as far as possible—and even, a little farther—conform to its conventions. Every day hers is the task of putting new wine in old bottles.

There may be trouble, Rosalie feels, with the advent into the home of that dream-set of china for which she is searching and which, so far, has evaded her, that rose-coloured dream-set that the rose-coloured tea-cosy has preceded. The same objections will be raised—at least, she will be told that already there are sufficient teacups in the house; that other, that they will *soil,* can scarcely be pertinent here. But they will be too fragile, or they will have handles that are too easily knocked off, or—something else. They shall not be considered, however, of that Rosalie is determined, like auntie's best set " too good for human nature's daily food," and kept, except on such occasions as baptisms or weddings, in glass cases!

But, perhaps—really I shouldn't wonder—seeing how criticism of that cosy affected the too-susceptible Rosalie, she may be just as nice as it is possible to be over those said teacups!

The problem of the rose-coloured tea-cosy is no uncommon one. Girls like to have things of their own. The love of pretty things was planted in them in pre-natal days as a tiny seed that, in most cases, should grow to exercise powerful influence upon them throughout life. Yet lest it sprout up too overwhelmingly, there is usually some counteracting influence imposed. In a flat of her own a girl has, perhaps, more opportunity of gratifying it even than in a home of her own—where a husband might prefer a cosy of a different colour! In her flat she alone has full say. Only in that case lack of the wherewithal is often not merely a counteracting influence but an effective deterrent. In any case, life is usually a compromise—and freedom can be worth more than a rose-coloured cosy.

And Auntie? I think something must be said for her, too. It isn't—not always, at any rate—that the love of pretty things deserts us as we grow older. But she sets more value on memories. She would have the old things about her, the old customs, the old people—those who are left. She would have the same clock ticking away on the wall, where it used to tick. She would have the same old rug before the fire—sometimes she refuses to see that it is growing threadbare. She would hear the same voices, and because some of them are silenced, she would cling all the more tenaciously to " the things that remain."

THE ROSE-COLOURED COSY

I have wandered far from the rose-coloured tea-cosy!
And yet, even seeing Auntie's point of view I feel that
Rosalie will be justified in using it one day.

A BABY'S SMILES

SHE is not quite two years old. She wears a white frock trimmed with blue ribbons. Her baby head is covered with soft silky hair of pale gold. The front lock persists in drooping into her eyes. The puny efforts of that tiny bit of blue ribbon are quite unable to restrain the wayward lock. The eyes, whose beauty it seeks to hide, are brightly and intensely blue. So recently opened upon this world, they find many things to observe and wonder at. Sometimes it would seem they are mystified. And a shadow strange and serious flits into them, and holds them steadfast because of something that they do not understand. But when the smile of recognition comes —it is a wonderful thing! So wonderful that it awakens smiles in older eyes, so serious and so worldly-wise that they scarcely ever now see anything to smile at.

There is surely much joy and laughter lying ahead in the years for Esmé Violet. Her plump, rosy cheeks seem to betoken it. She has passed much of her little life lying in her pram in the garden. Like the flowers, she has grown up to the advanced age of two!

Many are the things that she is interested in. Each day adds something to her store of knowledge. For Esmé Violet to live is to learn. She learned the other day that those real-looking roses on mummy's jumper were not for picking. They caught her eyes at once—bright things always do. The crowd of grown-ups, who are deceivers ever, stood around, egging her on :—" Pick a rose for me, Baby." So the tiny hand was outstretched, but the rose refused to be picked. A little look of disappointment came into the baby eyes. Esmé Violet looked round her crowd of admirers wonderingly. They were smiling. So she smiled too.

Already Esmé Violet is mistress of many feminine arts. She will come to you with outstretched arms, and when you have raised her to your lap, she will snuggle most restfully and confidingly against you.

But Esmé Violet has no intention of posing for any picture, however charming, if it demands that she remain passive. So she says, " Up ! " She stands upright on your knee. And the tiny hands go round your neck, and the touch of the baby fingers is so gentle and soft that already you are quite securely trammelled up in the snare she has laid for you. And then she says, " Eggies ! " And that puts an end to dreamy reverie, Esmé Violet's head on your shoulder, by the fire.

A journey to the next room is necessary, where she knows a wondrous collection of eggs is stored. These she is never tired of visiting. You bring her back, and, in a few minutes so exacting are her royal demands once she is sure of your allegiance, it must be done all over again ! These " eggies " mean much to her. She sometimes thinks in terms of eggs. A lady visitor the other day wore a necklace of beads of a shape and nature that

were strange to Esmé Violet. These she defined as
" red eggies! "

Before Esmé Violet came, Teddie was the pet and play-
thing of the household. A little shaggy terrier, he knew
his own importance, and wielded undisputed sway. It
might have been thought that he would resent this intrusion of another, to whom he must play second fiddle.
Teddie was useful for providing entertainment for any
odd moments that were found lying around. He was
always present at afternoon tea, and gracefully acknow-
ledged, by waggings of his tail, his gratitude for pieces of
bread and butter and cake that always came his way. So
superior, however, were the attractions of Esmé Violet,
that she provided entertainment, not only for idle
moments, but for every moment of the day. So, no doubt,
Teddie wondered. It took him a little while to get accustomed to the little stranger. But now they are firm
friends.

While Esmé Violet lies out in her pram, Teddie
slumbers beside her on the grass. One of the first words
she learned to say was " Dog ". One of the first noises
she learned to make was Teddie's expression of gratitude,
Teddie's way of saying " Thank you " when he sees you
donning your coat, and knows that he is sure of a walk.
Baby fingers may ruffle his hair; they may even snatch at
his tail. Teddie merely looks as if he liked it! So assured
are the conquests made by Esmé Violet.

Esmé Violet never questions the fact that you must be
interested in her and in all that pertains to her. She is
a queen and must be obeyed. You may just have started

a discussion that promises to be absorbing—though, of course, leading nowhere—on the Unemployment Problem, or you may even be hot in debate over the best recipes for making marmalade. These you must leave on one side, to worship at Esmé Violet's shrine. She has opened her drawer of treasures, and she passes one of them for your close inspection, and waits for the expressions of the admiration that is sure to come. Then she hands you another toy. And no matter how serious-minded a man of business you may be, however learned in the law, or in medicine or in things ecclesiastical, here you must become as a little child and try to see these woolly lamps and jingling rattles and dolls, dressed and undressed, with Esmé Violet's eyes. Otherwise, you are a failure!

When Esmé Violet journeys out into the big world in her pram, she is very observant. At first, when she began to talk, she could only express her appreciation of what she saw in monosyllables such as "Dog," "Boy," "Girl." Now the words are connecting themselves together. When she is playing quietly around, while others are talking, they think she is taking no notice. Then at unexpected moments comes out some stray word that she has caught. A lady addressed her several times one day as "Little Sunbeam." Esmé Violet seemed to be paying no attention. Then a whole fortnight afterwards mummy heard her muttering to herself "Little Sunbeam!" As one of her admirers asked wonderingly the other day: "How much of it all do babies such as she understand?"

AS OTHERS SEE US

I HAVE been shopping and have come home wearied and filled with a depressing sense of my own insignificance. It has been one of these days when everything has gone "contrairy." Even pussy, as she lies comfortably on my lap, has closed her eyes, caring little for my condition of disquieting egoism or the thoughts that keep surging through my mind. . . .

We are all, more or less, egoists. We tend to exaggerate our own importance. Around us the universe revolves. The other Egos, extraneous to our own special Ego, revolve with the universe.

The thought of it may inflate us with a sense of our own significance. Or it may merely make us conscious of our own unbolstered-up isolation. If the latter effect is produced, and we desire solace, we have only to study the answers given, through the newspapers and periodicals, to the shy young maiden who seeks a cure for self-consciousness and blushing: "Think of other people and not of yourself." In print it is advice easy enough to follow.

But if we are inflated? We do not seek a cure, but surely it is there, if we are observant enough to see it, in the complete indifference of other people. We may be flushed with some achievement. We may have emerged triumphantly from some examination or some political success. We may have secured a particularly becoming hat. We may have become engaged to be married. We may have won a large sum in a cross-word competition. But what does it matter to our charwoman or our postman? To the former we are merely a destructive agent that undoes her white-washing labours. To the latter, a private source of complaint because of the number of our returned MSS. To our cobbler we are nothing more than " the lady that belongs to these shoes "!

What does our cross-word success matter to the waitress who serves our lunch in a North Bridge restaurant? She is not concerned with individuals, with their propensities for soaring or for cringing. She deals with knives and forks, not with men and women. Hers is the all-absorbing business of keeping three or four tables " going " simultaneously. To her, as to the charwoman, men and women are destructive agents. They mess up her tables. They change her carefully created cosmos of neatly arranged silver and glass and linen into a chaos of half-empty plates and soiled serviettes, broken-up cakes and stained table-cloths. And she, having provided all her other tables with their soup or their hors d'œuvres, their curried mutton or their peach Melba, looks not to the consumption of the same. No, once again she is bringing that disordered table back into the condition in which there is a place for everything and everything occupies that place.

That done, off she rushes again, fetching and carrying, hunting round for a specially desired tipsy cake or an

AS OTHERS SEE US

éclair with chocolate icing instead of pink, changing a cup of tea for a cup of cocoa to suit her customer's changed state of mind. Need one wonder that she remains unconscious that her customer is excited because she has been left a fortune or because she has just received news that she is a grandmother?

Outside in Princes Street Gardens there are crocuses, purple, white, and yellow, clinging to the banks. They are of the spring-time, speaking of the brightness that comes when the dark night of winter is past. The sparrows know that they are there, though they have eyes only for the yellow crocuses. But does she know? Do we ever think about it? From our egocentric standpoint I am afraid we don't. If to her, we are the agents who disarrange her tables, to us she is merely a fetching and carrying agent. To us, in many cases, she might as well be a machine. And yet, perhaps, even she, like Guinevere, has wandered in the spring-time

"Under groves that looked a paradise
Of blossom, over sheets of hyacinth
That seemed the heavens upbreaking through the
earth."

We may have come straight from the production of some weighty contribution to philosophic thought, but what does mademoiselle, our milliner, think of it? It is not with the inside of our head, but with the outside, that she is concerned. To see that outside crowned with an adequate piece of millinery, that is her business. Perhaps she even finds in our beneficent mood an opportunity for getting rid of some unwanted model that has long encumbered her salon. So she fetches it, and adjusts it, and pokes it, and pulls it, and admires it from a distance, and assures madame that it is the very hat for her—that nothing more particularly adapted to madame's style could possibly have seen the light of day. But madame, no doubt, sees through the little scheme, and remains unsusceptible to the young lady's blandishments.

And so mademoiselle, too, like the waitress, proceeds with the business of fetching and carrying. The tall crowned cloche hat in royal blue, with its high trimming of anemones; the tiny scarlet hat, beset with yellow stars; the large gracefully drooping model in black that has caught a side-spray of full-blown cerise roses and holds them half above and half below the brim; these, and others, too, she fetches and fits to the head; she finds them discarded, and she fetches others. Her philosophy is not concerned with treatises; it is one of physical endurance.

The car conductor, as he punches the tickets and collects the pennies of all and sundry, does it matter to him that his little company includes learned dignitaries of the Church, university dons, men in working clothes, ladies of fashion wearing these hats that they have newly acquired, and others, who know no such thing as fashion, wearing none at all? Not much—unless there is a collision, when his passengers will be sorted out and accorded the prominence due to them. To him they are units who offer him pennies, or, to the detriment of his temper, half-crowns and Treasury notes. They are units

AS OTHERS SEE US

that are prone to lodge complaints and to argue about their rights. Only that and nothing more.

Our dumb friends—are they overwhelmed with a sense of our importance, even of the importance of humanity in general over the canine or the feline kind? Not in the least. Human beings exist to minister to their comfort—especially, perhaps, is it true of the pussy-cat tribe. New hats and cross-word prowess, University distinctions and fat bank accounts, count for nothing here. Human beings provide laps in which pussy can nestle and repose to her heart's content. They open the back door, and if pussy, seeing that rain is falling, draws back and seeks the front, hoping that different weather conditions may prevail there—they open that, too! They fill saucers with milk. They push pussy's stool closer to the fire. They pet her when she seeks consolation. They learn from her that it is she that matters —no mere isolated human units! She pays them, it is true, a slight tribute in the matter of purrs and caresses.

It is a world that is humbling to the individual, that quickly reduces feelings of self-importance, through the medium of resentment, perhaps, to a sense that one is merely tolerated. And those who have not passed through the process—having daily encountered an array of charwomen and lift-boys and tram-conductors and waitresses and the rest—have surely benefited little by their transit through life. Perhaps some modern religious sects may even hold that they will have to start it all over again.

THE QUIET HOLIDAY

It was morning. A bright, sunny, summery morning. The tiniest little breeze was just stirring the branches, setting the leaves of the chestnut tree rustling. Its tall pink and white candlesticks had already disappeared.

To the little girl who swung to and fro under the chestnut arbour the fact was one for regret. She had loved these candlesticks. But the white petals and the pink had fallen softly, like confetti, to the ground, and over that flowery carpet she had swung to and fro in the evenings, just for a little while after school and before she went in to wrestle with the vulgar fractions that she thought so thoroughly deserved their name.

Now the holidays had come, and Mona could swing all day long if so it pleased her. At the moment it did please her—very much so!

For Mona did not like school. If I told you why, I should merely smear my canvas for a perfect summer day's picture. It held—yes, really!—things that in Mona's eyes were considerably worse even than vulgar fractions. It was a place to escape from on *any* pretext whatever. (As Mona's view of school life is, in these days, so unpopular, it may be possible that you will concede her, on that account, a special claim upon your attention!)

Presently Mona allowed the swing to come to rest be-

THE QUIET HOLIDAY

neath the green branches of the chestnut tree. She remembered that she had promised to feed the rabbits—why,
there was Snowball stretching her paws right up the side
of the wire net enclosure—her method of asking for her
breakfast. Mona took up the little basket that was stained
over and over, even as were her little hands, with the juice
of dandelions, and she set off down the little country lane,
sandwiched so tight between two encroaching hedges.
She knew just where the " sour leeks " grew, where the
dandelions were milkiest, and where the tares clambered
up the hedges, securing themselves with their tiny tendrils,
so that their purply-blue flowers might make the finest
show and have the best vantage point. It seemed a pity
to tear down these blue flowers, but Mona suddenly remembered Snowball's hunger—and Snowball did love the
flowers of tares! So the blossoms fell beneath the relentless hand. And Snowball, when she returned home, was
perfectly satisfied, and ate her breakfast without any fear
of subsequent indigestion.

Mona put down her little basket, and paused for a
moment. What should she do next? She was entirely
dependent upon herself for entertainment. Mother was
busy. She looked a little regretfully at the swing. She
thought, with longing of her story-book that told of a
whole big family of children who had the loveliest times
together—what games one could play if one had brothers
and sisters! Mona gave just the tiniest little sigh. But,
after all, she had her dream-children for companions.
Yes, they should accompany her now, this very moment,
while she weeded her garden.

So she collected her little spade and her little rake, and she hung the little basket once again on her arm. She opened the garden door, such an old, creaky, antiquated door, but it prevented beggars who came to the back door from ever seeing inside the garden! She walked past the little inquisitive faces of the wild pansies, and past the gean tree whose fruit was hard and bitter, and past the raspberry canes that refused to produce raspberries at all, and past the old-fashioned blush roses that looked in at the drawing-room window, and past—oh, quite a lot of other interesting things. But why enumerate all the pebbles on the beach?

Having passed them all, she arrived at her own little plot of land, and surveyed the scene with a feeling that things were far from being as her eye would see them. The rockets—yes they stood upright certainly, and she liked their pale colour and their elusive scent; and her Sweet William had upholstered its flowers correctly in lines of maroon and white. But how sick-looking even the pansies seemed, and her two carnations were positively wilting, and the little scarlet geranium, that father gave her, stood before her, a brown skeleton thing, unlovely in death. Mona's heart suffered a severe pang over that geranium. Of course, it was her own fault. She had read " Little Women "—or was it Angela Brazil?—instead of watering it.

Nothing on earth—or under it!—could save it now, but she should make amends, she vowed, to the carnations and the red daisies and the pansies. So she started digging with her little spade. Presently, however, she laid it down, finding her hands more effective as weed-removers, and as she rooted up the chick-weed and laid the groundsel low, she played with her dream children.

There were so many of them. Eva, who could do vulgar fractions, and sweep and dust and do all kinds of nice things for other people as well. And Elsie, who was a madcap and climbed trees and ran along the tops of walls; and Tom and Harry, who were always playing games, and did not despise their sisters for joining in; and Millie, who had the loveliest kitten; and the baby, who did nothing but look sweet and angelic all the time. And Mona saw herself arriving at their house one morning, and all of them coming out to welcome her. There was Eva to take her hat away, and Elsie to lead her off, and the boys to play the loveliest game of rounders, and Millie's kitten and the baby to admire. And then, in a corner, screened from all the others, she and Elsie were telling each other the most enchanting of secrets—yes, the very things that she never told to anybody else!

She paused just then for an instant, because the rose had pricked her finger. Then she tugged at a thistle, and as it came up, a great fleshy worm came crawling across the ground in her direction. Mona drew back in repulsion. No, she could never grow accustomed to worms! It was they who gave to gardening its unpleasant side—why were they created? She did not mind spiders, but she detested earwigs. . . . Where was she? Oh, yes, just whispering to Elsie that she had heard the very strangest noise in her bedroom one night—a ghost, without any mistake. Then Elsie told her that she had actually seen a ghost, and when Mona's eyes began to glower and grow big, she added, that at least she thought so—only—only—(Mona stuck for an explanation)—perhaps, it had been the moonlight shining on the wall. Then the girls had taken her into the house and shown her their new party frocks, just the colours of the sweet peas in father's part of the garden, pink and mauve and blue, and—but, oh, there was mother calling her.

She dropped her little spade and ran in to lunch, and to tell her mother, " I have been talking to my children ". And mother smiled—just a little wistfully.

In the afternoon Mona swung to her heart's content beneath the chestnut tree, and put on, in her dreams, the party frocks, first the blue one, then the mauve, then the rose. In the evening she read and read, only pausing to give Snowball her evening meal, to bring out her little watering-can and seek to refresh the drooping carnations and the tired daisies and the wearied pansies. . . .

Not much in her day, do I hear you say? Or was it, " Poor child, I'm sorry for her! " Perhaps you expected her story to lead up to some spectacular event, staged amidst a glare of colours? But why? Mona was wise enough to make just the best that she could of her holiday and her escape from vulgar fractions. Aren't we all—you and I and all of us—trying to follow her example at this very moment?

THE LADY IN GREY

To the Lady in Grey I go from time to time, in search of encouragement when the days become, perhaps, a little meaningless. She lives in a beautiful house beyond the Dean Bridge : she calls it the House of Far Distances. It gives her a view of one of the main roads entering the city; it gives her, too, peeps at cornfields and at the sea, at tenements, back-gardens, the crests of wooded hills and the masts of ships in port. She is an invalid, and her whole time is passed between two rooms. A writer of books, she is generous in sharing with others the thoughts that come to her in her loneliness.

The Lady in Grey—until the other day I had not seen her for quite a long time, for she has been often ill—will, she tells me, soon be a Lady in Grey no longer. Her hair, so she explained to me, is becoming grey, and along with her pale face, it makes her look too dull altogether. So she is thinking of changing her colour scheme to a blue one—for that, I think, is the colour that she loves most of all. The walls of the room where she passes most of her time have recently been changed into soft azure attire; her bed has a blue cover; and her blue dream is now complete save that she would have the variegated cretonne covers on the chairs and couch also changed into that colour, freely sprayed over with primroses. For blue, she holds, the heaven's own colour, is entirely restful and satisfactory.

The title of the Lady in Grey proved a misnomer even upon this recent occasion, for her *robe de chambre*—I hope that she will excuse my mentioning it—was of pale blue, and a fleecy shawl, like a little handful of sky, lying apart, echoed its blueness. The teacups, too, were blue. Only the lamp-shade was different, being apricot-coloured, lined with rich pink to make a brightening glow for eyes that need the refreshment of colour.

Just for a little over an hour was I allowed to talk to her—I am afraid that I sadly transgressed the rule—it was little enough time when all the affairs, not only of the last three months, but of the whole of life, with even perhaps a little forward glimpse into eternity, came crowding into it! It passed all too soon.

As usual, the flowers came to bear her company in enforced retirement—one of her young friends has christened her the Flower Lady. On the table beside her the carnations were of that shade of satisfying pink which is the most lovable of all; with them and with the blue irises was mixed the summery, snow-like spray of gypsophila, a tiny vase holding some precious wood-violets. Another floral contribution had a country-garden look about it, which, it is possible, may bring its appeal of the wild to contrast with the sophisticated florists' bouquets. It held pansies and pinks, lupins and London Pride and stocks, all tight packed together, also a single crimson peony. It was long since a peony had come to visit the Lady in Grey, as she had been remarking just a short time before its unexpected arrival.

The whole " art " of a day for her is, as she explained to me, to try not to get tired. One of the secrets of her cheerfulness in her invalidism is that, just as she makes the most of the flowers that come to her, knowing their hearts, so does she extract the secrets of her visitors as individuals. When you leave her you cannot help feeling that she knows a great deal about you, and a good deal more than you have ever told her! Confidences that you have never confided to her are hers, and the knowledge of that comes with a little feeling of surprise to those, who, walking in more crowded ways, are accustomed to give each other but a casual glance and pass on.

When her visitors have gone I feel that she lies and dreams about them, comparing them, contrasting them, fitting them into some scheme or philosophy of which they themselves have not the remotest inkling. It is not always just quite easy to follow her into the labyrinths of her generalities, the fault being ours entirely, for we who are continually rushing about and busying ourselves too much with concrete things and concrete instances, do not generalise over-much. So that it is good to know that there are those ready and willing to do our philosophising for us.

The care of our possessions—that was one topic that cropped up for discussion. The handling of the things that we love, careful that no little blemish shall mar their perfection. It is doubtless a care that can be exaggerated, and that must ever be remembered by those who have been warned to lay up for themselves no treasure upon earth. Yet how it hurts to see our cherished belongings roughly touched by unloving fingers! Even to see these same fingers treat their own possessions thus grates upon all those who love the beautiful. The Lady in Grey quoted for me two extreme instances, from her own experience, of an exquisite old china bowl having been taken by a nurse to make a poultice, of a valuable Indian shawl having had a hole burned in it through being called upon by some ununderstanding person to do duty as a lampshade! Happy are those of us who have escaped being the victims of such atrocities.

It takes all kinds of people to make a world—the sooner that we realise the truth of that which is so often upon our lips as a mere catchword the better. Yet those lacking reverence can be as much out of place in a sickroom as the proverbial bull in the china shop. When one has to lie apart, and play the passive *rôle* all the time, it is no wonder if one's feelings become somewhat acute under such provocation.

Among her most frequent visitors is Memory. I wonder, indeed, if Memory ever takes her leave. Memory leads her back over the ways she walked in once, and, even lying in bed, one can take the most delightful excursions, more wonderful, indeed, than most of us take nightly to dreamland.

To the Lady in Grey her women-friends mean much. She would never be numbered among those of smaller natures and petty jealousies, who argue against the reliability of women friends. They come to her in her solitude, each bringing something of her own personality, to linger on behind when, in visible form, she has departed. Among them are numbered, if I mistake not, an artist, a novelist, a poet, and when they do not come, for the demands that life makes upon us all are exacting, their letters do duty instead—and I hope these may be letters that take the recipient out into primrose-scented ways, the clover fields, and the happy autumn woods. We have to lie aside from Life—" to feel," as she says, " life a great reality, yet just out of reach "—to realise what the coming of these visitors, these letters, means. Having escaped the weighted bonds of sickness and weariness, it is so easy to forget! . . .

But it was time to go, to leave the Lady in Grey to her flowers and her thoughts. Nothing of tremendous import had been said, you may interpolate. But impressions last longer than mere words; memories matter more. And the picture that I carried with me had a wonderfully brightening effect on the rainy street outside and the sea of umbrellas that made it duller still.

PICTURES IN DAILY LIFE

How often do we find that artists are forced to express themselves through another medium of art than that of picture-painting, simply because there is no money in the business, they tell us. Mr. Bernard Shaw, at the unveiling of certain frescoes in the Tate Gallery, suggested a remedy. He finds it in a return to the old habit of covering the actual walls of public buildings and private houses with paintings, in a return to the old idea that the artist should be called in as a workman to carry out the work. So that by paying a moderate weekly salary anyone can have his whole house painted instead of buying expensive pictures.

There is a good deal to be said for Mr. Shaw's suggested remedy! Then we should be able to change our decorations as often as, at present, we change our wall-paper. For I scarcely think that Mr. Shaw would intend these pictures to remain on the walls until they are in the condition, say of Leonardo da Vinci's " Last Supper " at Milan. That being so, the artist's lot would be worse than it is now.

Many of us refrain from buying pictures because our walls are already well covered. Not, it may be, with the pictures that we should prefer to see thereon; not with the subjects or the colours that are our own soul's choice; but with the pictures from which, for sentimental reasons, we cannot part. They may have been handed down to us. They may have been given to us as wedding presents— a dangerous choice! But there they are, and there they must remain, while the pictures which we might, by a careful balancing of coins together, purchase to replace them, go unbought, space in our houses being a strictly rationed commodity.

It is not good for us to live all the time with the same pictures. Far from it. Have I not, for many a year, from my favourite corner of the fireplace, gazed into the stern, reproachful eyes of my great-aunt Jane, while Gladys Cooper or Mary Pickford would, at least, have offered the excuse of beauty for thus continually thrusting themselves upon me! Have I not, for the same number of winter nights and summer afternoons, merely had to change my angle to be confronted by an old-world print in black and white so unattractive that no one has ever sought to unravel its mysteries, the while I would have my thoughts decoyed and set awandering down ferny lanes and glades blue with forget-me-nots? Oh, it is all quite wrong—isn't it?

We ought to change our pictures sometimes—and, by that, I don't mean merely to put great-aunt Jane where the black and white is, and *vice-versa*. Let all of them be banished, and put an entirely new set on the walls, until a sentimental conscience begins to prick too sharply, and great-aunt Jane and all the rest come back—for a time.

But, from a practical point of view, it really isn't possible. Modern architects make no allowances for such whimsical up-turnings. Isn't cupboard space a luxury pined for in vain by the bungalow housewife of to-day? If great-aunt Jane leaves her accustomed corner, she must overcrowd somebody's bedroom, or hide behind the piano, or stand with her face to the wall, in a corner of the hall. But the owner of the bedroom objects to her company therein, and the charwoman objects to it any-where else. And so the poor artists must starve! It would appear that there is a good deal to be said for Mr. Bernard Shaw's idea of having artists to paint our walls. Nobody would be inconvenienced.

Private initiative being impossible, could not public enterprise do something in the way of housing these orphan pictures that are homeless? What about an agency for lending out pictures, run on the lines of a lending library? It might start by helping the newly-married, whose walls save for a few unfortunate wedding presents, are innocent of decoration of this kind. For a moderate annual subscription one could then have one's pictures changed when desired. The problem of space would be abolished—there would be no over-crowding into bedroom or bathroom.

Of course, we should have to wait our turn for those pictures that were greatly in demand. And if there be one particular masterpiece that we desire to hang over the sideboard at our Christmas party, it would be well, of course, to order it in time. Imagine our feelings on being told " Oh, the ' Innocence of Spring-Time '? That is already booked for Mrs. Whyte-Black's reception "

—our hated rival. And that picture was just of the right size, too, to cover the damp patch on the wall!

Apart from catering for private households, the picture agency would hold out special terms, or I am mistaken, to such like public people as doctors and dentists and lawyers and to institutions such as schools, the Post Office, Inland Revenue offices, and railway companies. Some doctors' and dentists' waiting-rooms, I grant you, have quite respectable pictures on their walls; some have not. But in their case, again, it is monotony that I am up against. If I wait in the doctor's outer chamber, till it please him to admit me to his *sanctum sanctorum* to have a finger lanced, under a picture representing Mary Queen of Scots with her head laid on the block, I should prefer when next I return for a prescription for a cold, to gaze at a picture of " Hope Triumphant." Railway stations by way of their gay-coloured posters, have certainly of recent years done their bit in helping the artists, but class-rooms, offices, hairdressing saloons, have plenty of deficiencies to make good in this connection.

I might have added tea-rooms, also, had I not in mind a particular tea-room in Edinburgh that sets an excellent example from an artistic point of view. Artists have a chance to show their pictures there, not as in an exhibition, but as part of the ordinary setting; and this is all to the good, for Mr. Shaw would have pictures in refreshment rooms. The pictures are changed every three months, I understand.

Why are exhibitions often so disappointing, so flat?

Isn't it because we set out with the set purpose of being impressed by something extraordinary, having paid our shilling of entry-money? And in life the beauty that really impresses is that that steals upon us unawares, and for which we pay nothing. That is why, rather than going on conducted tours that set out on purpose to see something, it is better to wander round by ourselves and let things make their own impressions upon us.

I have Mr. Richard King with me in this thought. Does he not write, in his "One Quiet Evening":— "That wonder-sense which we hope to remember all our lives as a kind of Moment of Transfiguration, we are convinced must be in the vicinity of the Pyramids, or round the islands of the Pacific, or in Athens, or Herculaneum, or in Seville on Easter Monday. Never, oh, never, in a quiet by-lane in Surrey, or in a cottage garden in Sussex, or near the Round Pond in Kensington Gardens, or outside our bedroom window as we draw down the blinds on a moonlight night." He goes on to speak of the disappointment produced by the crowded beauty of the Louvre; the satisfaction, on coming out, to find the Arc de Triomphe caught in a blaze of sunset glory, the Champs Elysées a shining river of gold. It is the impression made by unexpected beauty that remains—the picture in the tea-room, not in the exhibition hall.

Do not dismiss my plea for more pictures in our daily life, if only on the lending system—even wedding veils are often "lent"—as entirely unworkable. It is so disappointing to the artists to paint on and paint on, if their pictures are only to occupy much-wanted space in their own houses. These same pictures could do so much to brighten our own mental outlook and that of the public generally—if only great-aunt Jane were ousted, or the bare spaces filled up!

DREAM-CHILDREN

TO-DAY two children came to tea. I hope that Miss Seventeen will not be offended at being included in such a category, since childhood, after all, is merely a comparative term. Miss Seven, of course, can offer no objection. They have flower names—no, not Lily or Daisy. "They tell me flower-names are out of fashion," said Miss Seventeen, but I do not think she allowed the thought to disturb her equanimity.

Miss Seventeen has decided literary and artistic leanings, and Miss Seven seeks to follow in her sister's footsteps. So far, however, not being able to manipulate a pen, she is obliged to dictate her letters for transmission. Games, too, are a favourite pursuit of Miss Seventeen, so, of course, Miss Seven is, even already, learning to wield her golf clubs.

Gardening interests them. Raking up the autumn leaves that too quickly litter up the garden is the daily duty of little Miss Seven. "But I have a garden of my own," she announced, with pride, and when questioned as to the plants that bloomed therein, she exclaimed "A potato!"

Miss Seven has at least a nodding acquaintance with elves and similar mysterious creatures. Perhaps it was only my fancy that saw a suggestion of elfishness in herself, a right mischievous look that steals over her little face when she thinks that she is going to spring something in the nature of a surprise upon her grown-up friends!

When they had gone a sudden quietness stole upon us, as though something really vital had gone out of the room. Had they been among us, or were they but the children of a dream? . . .

Out of the silence one began to see other dream-children rising up like unto, yet different from, those of Charles Lamb. Something of the atmosphere of the storybook world of childhood began to steal back. Grave Alices and laughing Allegras, and Ediths with golden hair drifted back unsummoned, unexpected. In the firelight they seemed to be meeting and mingling in a dancing shadowy crowd.

We all remember the delights of the story that was written about a large family of children. There was such a snug, comfortable kind of atmosphere about such a family. The members of it were so useful in rubbing each other's corners down; no wonder nerves were heard of less in these days.

The modern fashion of a family of one, two, at most three, from the story-book point of view is surely a tendency to be regretted, even if inevitable. We shall have to draw more and more upon the dream-children to people the silences, we of a generation that has loved Meg and Jo, Beth and Amy.

From among these shadowy children who came crowding into the firelight, definite shapes seemed to arise. And, of course, stretching out welcoming hands, they led me back to the scenes among which they used to live and move and have their being. I passed, led by one of them, to a house that seemed to be the happy prototype of all the story-books of girlhood, since it held a family of six golden-haired girls. There was much that was companionable and intimate about the scene when they were all gathered, of a winter evening, about the tea-table, chattering gaily all the time, each voice inserting itself whenever it saw a loophole for entry into the conversation—and it was difficult to find it! Especially as there is always one who will succeed in talking the others down! Nor is it, by any means, always the eldest —she was usually too busy attending to the needs of the younger children, in proper story-book style.

Always when I think of these children there are apples in the picture. Jo, you remember, usually had apples with her in that attic of hers, where she wrote her stories. Apples are such comforting accompaniments of life in almost any circumstances, so that a picture of perfect domestic bliss ought to hold them as it does the black cat on the hearth! These children fitted most admirably into a Christmas picture of the cosy, curtained room kind.

Amy, like that other Amy, was the youngest. She was very pretty, with golden hair that floated about her shoulders, as hair did in these days. She always had a sunny smile, and I still see her sitting at the fire with her picture book in front of her. "Amy just sits about making everybody feel happy," said an older sister as she stroked her hair. I know you would love to hear what happened to Amy, who was so well fitted to play the princess of a fairy tale, but I am not going to enlighten you. You must be content to leave her among the dream-children.

There is another little girl, belonging to a much older generation, who looks at me out of a quaint little old-fashioned frame, in which she stands beside her seated older sister. Her eyes are wide open; her face, with its fresh, innocent expression, has not even dimly glimpsed the varied possibilities of the years in front, and her arms, stretching out of their tiny puffed sleeves, are bare. Her short hair clusters about her neck. Her older sister's long dress is striped with the stripes—to us so inartistic—loved by that generation, though they tended to obscure one's personality.

I think that she would be rather shy about joining in the dancing, that serious-looking little pictured girl. At any rate she could never come to it with the care-free ease of my golden-haired Amy. I see her playing hide-and-seek, with that quiet, mysterious smile of hers. But perhaps I am mistaken, after all; she might become quite wildly excited and be taken entirely " out of herself."

Her chief occupation, indulged in in her humble but so happy home, was the cutting out of paper figures. Every available scrap of paper she stored up for that purpose. With her paper and scissors she hid herself in the attic upstairs under the eaves of her tiny home, and cut, and cut, and cut!

Then there is another little pictured girl who has

grown up with a friend of mine. She was a companion of nursery days, raising herself by means of a book beside her friend the collie, and proudly exclaiming, "I's 'e biggest." She wasn't, of course, but that merely added to the charm of it. She still looks down from my friend's bedroom wall. Yes, certainly, she should join these dancing children.

A little boy with his wondering brown eyes, who always asked. "Why?" A girl with straight fair hair who wrote stories for her dolls. A dark-eyed beauty who used to sing gay little snatches of songs, and who looked a perfect picture, when her dark hair was piled up, Japanese fashion, in fancy dress, and she was wrapt in a gaily-flowered kimono. They are all dancing in that gay jing-a-ring. . . .

Just at this season of Armistice Day, with its poppies of remembrance, I see so many of these dream-children coming back to revisit their mothers. Always when the mothers, grey-haired now, and rather sad-looking, sit alone in the firelight I think they are looking at these dancing children—that is why they are so wistful. On Armistice Day the shapes become less dimly outlined, each stands out very clearly, and they leave off their dancing, and come to her, one by one, as she sits alone, placing their hands confidingly in hers . . . the boys she has lost . . . the girls whose lives have been shadowed through the tragedy of war. . . . They speak to her, across the separating and devastating years, of their playthings and their lessons, bringing to her, as they used to do, their little sorrows, their childish joys.

And I think that it is just because these dream-children come to her then, out of the silence and the gloom, as she sits alone, that she is able, with fresh courage, next day, to face the empty stretch of life anew.

THE NEW DANCE FROCK

DID you think the task of buying the new dance frock an easy one? May I venture to disillusion you? . . .

The story is that as related to me by my friend Celia, who went as spectator and adviser with Rosalind, who was to select the frock. And, lest you think the name Rosalind a misnomer, I would explain that it is not hers as a possessor of the boyish figure, now fast, so the dress-experts assure us, becoming extinct. Nor is it hers because she ever showed evidence of any overpowering compulsion to don the doublet and hose. Hers it is merely because she played the leading part in the little drama. . . .

Celia's story, then.

* * * *

9.55 a.m. Scene, a dress parlour *chez* Madame Violette in George Street. The distinction between a parlour and a shop is not a tremendously fine one, but seems to exist in the fact that the former shows less sign of merchandise and mundane commercialism. There is an atmosphere of greater secrecy about it, of hidden mysteries screened from the casual eye. It shares something of that wider difference that separates the Rue de la Paix from the meaner end of the Rue de Rivoli, Bond Street from the Kensington High Street. Here are a few models skilfully disposed—one feels that even an additional one might convey a suggestion of vulgar ostentatiousness.

" Madame desires a black dance frock? Yes, certainly, black *is* the colour this season. Everywhere one sees it. No, but certainly it is not considered ageing. Did not Madame remark that the younger of the two Spanish Princesses wore black, while her mother, Queen Ena, appeared in white? " Rosalind is reassured that black and none other is certainly the colour for her dance frock.

So the cases are opened, and the black robes are extracted. There is one that is garish, with red trappings. " Madame wears red? " A decided negative dismisses that particular model, and another with heliotrope embellishments is similarly waved aside. That leaves a robe of soft satin, a frilly lace one, and a " renovation " dress of taffetas, stiff and rustling. You know what a renovation dress is? It is a sort of sheath, with close relationship to a dressing-gown, that parts in the middle to display your last season's evening dress. Practical, but in Rosalind's eyes inartistic, especially when composed of the taffetas that is quite capable of standing alone.

The frilly lacy dress is tried on, but it is found to be wholly inadequate—the correct word. It is the dress for a little ballet girl—if she didn't prefer a white one. The satin dress, at first, is frowned upon. Isn't satin—well—inclined to be too old? Oh, but Madame is wholly mistaken. Madame has certainly been misinformed. Madame has not. . . ? Of course, Rosalind knows that she meant to say—" used her eyes." She, the modiste, is so tired of georgette—has she not handled nothing else for years? Did she not always love the softness of satin folds for her personal wear? Rosalind relents when she hears that the satin is soft. That dress, however, is inadequate too, and could never become an affair of straight lines—when applied to herself.

Madame then produces her *pièce de resistance*. True, it is an afternoon gown, but the sleeves can easily be extracted, and they will be so useful later. This gown is a fairy-like thing, despite the fact that it, too, shows dressing-gown or overall ancestry in the method of its fastening. It is composed of filmy black, on which are embroidered all kinds of charming little flowers in red and purple, blue and green, and yellow. Daintily they climb up its lace; delicately, as an elf upon a rosebud, they poise upon the drooping foam of these lacy sleeves that are to be placed upon the shelf. A dream-frock . . . but, of course . . . too expensive. Sadly, Rosalind lays it on one side, and puts on her hat and coat and takes up her gloves. She is disappointed, chilled, and a sense of inferiority is getting busily to work. Celia remains merely complacent. The spectator sees most of the comedy.

If Madame comes when there is a dress show on, Violette assures her, she is certain to find something to suit her. Rosalind finds her spirits not greatly elevated—isn't the Whyte-Brownes' affair next Friday?

* * * *

Time, 10.55 a.m. An ordinary shop in North Bridge. More inadequate black dresses. More of stiff taffetas, and ballet-like dimensions and make-up; unlonged-for satins, unpined-for chenilles—though "they are quite the rage, Madam, and much less expensive than they were last season."

Must Madam have a black frock? Now there is a beautiful robe of pink, of orange, of scarlet——?

Rosalind departs, with Celia in her wake.

*   *   *   *

Time, 11.55 a.m. Scene, another ordinary shop—by "ordinary" I merely imply not a parlour or a salon or a tea-room (they give you tea now at dress-shows), or anything extraordinary—in Princes Street. More inadequate black dresses. More frilly, ballet ones. More chenille embossed velvet ones—"But, Madam, I assure you quite young girls are wearing them everywhere. The ball-rooms are full of them. They are also much worn in colour." An orange model is produced, and is quickly hustled by Rosalind into the obscurity from which it emerged. (Of course, I know she was always prone to contrariety, and sometimes I have little sympathy with her. Her name should have been Mary.)

Evening dresses repulsed, the afternoon gowns again came in for an innings. The sleeves can easily be taken out. . . . Madam will find them so useful when she wishes to wear the gown as an afternoon one. Rosalind feels that, by that time, fashion may well demand a different type of sleeve, but she lets that pass. There is one whose lines fall as lines ought to fall according to a Euclidean definition of the line that is straight. It is of accordion-pleated crêpe-de-chine. Its border round the skirt is of rich, broad silky lace. Its shoulders are of similar lace. Its sleeves that are to be discarded, also fall in the requisite splash of foamy lace. . . .

It is equal to supporting and displaying an under-dress of any colour chosen to ring the changes.

Rosalind at once recognizes that it is the dress for her, though it appears to be over-adequate. So the fitter comes to raise the skirt and lower the neck, to fit it in here and let it out there, to pin up these unwanted sleeves, and again to assure Madam of their future utility.

And Rosalind rests content though I know quite well that had the fitter applied the word " slender " to another frock it would probably have been hers.

Celia thinks so, too.

But, of course . . . the sleeves will be so useful?